THE SCOTTISH LEGAL TRADI

NEW ENLARGED EDITION

THE
SALTIRE SOCIETY

THE
STAIR SOCIETY

The Scottish Legal Tradition

New enlarged edition

by

MICHAEL C. MESTON, MA, LLB, JD
Professor of Private Law, University of Aberdeen

W. DAVID H. SELLAR, BA, LLB
Senior Lecturer in Scots Law, University of Edinburgh

The Rt. Hon. LORD COOPER, LLD
Late President of the Court of Session

Foreword by
The Rt. Hon. the LORD MACKAY OF CLASHFERN, PC, LLD
Lord High Chancellor of Great Britain

Afterword by
The Hon. LORD DERVAIRD, MA, LLB
Dickson Minto Professor of Company Law, University of Edinburgh

Edited by
Scott Crichton Styles, MA, LLB

Jointly Published by
THE SALTIRE SOCIETY and THE STAIR SOCIETY
Edinburgh 1991

This edition first published 1991

British Library Cataloguing in Publication Data
Cooper, Thomas MacKay
The Scottish Legal Tradition.—New enl. ed.
1. Scotland. Legal Tradition
I. Meston, M.C. (Michael Charles). II. Sellar, W. David H.
III. Cooper, Thomas Mackay
344.1107

ISBN 0-85411-045-3

The publisher gratefully acknowledges subsidy from the Scottish Arts Council towards the publication of this volume.

The illustration on the cover is reproduced from
'Advocates' in *A Series of Original Portraits and Caricature Etchings by the late John Kay* . . . Edinburgh 1837–38.

Designed by Ruari McLean

Printed and bound by the Alden Press, Oxford

iv

Contents

Foreword

It is surely a very remarkable fact that 280 years after the Treaty of Union under which the Parliaments of Scotland and England were united into the Parliament of the United Kingdom the Scottish Legal System and the principles under which it operates are as strong today as they were at the time of the Union.

The English Common Law System has prevailed not just in England and Wales but in the United States and throughout most of the Commonwealth. This wide geographical spread has generated a huge number of cases over the years which has given the common law the strength and variety which results from having considered nearly every conceivable legal problem. Compared to the worldwide scope of the common law the Scottish Legal System is a small jurisdiction and as a consequence of this the number of Scottish decisions is relatively small. Naturally, when a Scots lawyer is confronted with a new problem he will look to see what solution has been reached in England or in the other common law jurisdictions, but it does not necessarily follow that Scots law will accept the same solution.

Likewise, in many areas of law Parliament has intervened to legislate not only for England and Wales but also for Scotland. Where it has done so in branches of the law where the distinctive Scottish system differs from that in England and Wales the legislation is either separate or included in provisions that contain Scottish adaptations. In this way the distinctive principles of the Scottish system have been preserved even where Parliament has legislated a policy which has been adopted for the United Kingdom as a whole.

Maintaining these distinctive principles has been the responsibility both of the judiciary of Scotland and its community of legal scholars. Lord Cooper was eminent both as a judge and as a scholar.

I first saw Lord Cooper in his judicial role when I went into the Court of Session as a student in the early 1950s. I had already seen him when he came to St Andrews in the late 1940s as the chairman of a committee set up to investigate the relationship between the part of the University of St Andrews in Dundee and the part in St Andrews. In his professional dress, black jacket, striped trousers and bowler hat he cut an impressive figure, businesslike without being in any way pompous although he was the head of the Scottish judiciary.

The next time I saw Lord Cooper he was sitting as Lord President of the Court of Session presiding over the First Division of that court hearing an appeal. The question was whether the case should be sent to trial by jury or before a judge sitting alone. I was impressed by the calm dignity of Lord Cooper which gave him complete control of the court without in any way inhibiting the argument, and his interventions in the debate were always beautifully expressed. One of the counsel in the case was later to be Lord Emslie, himself to be the Lord President of the Court of Session. At one point when Mr Emslie was waxing eloquent on the inadequacies of the pursuer's case Lord Cooper intervened: "Mr Emslie, if this case goes before a jury you will bring tears to their eyes".

Lord Cooper lived in a lovely house on the south side of Edinburgh and on one occasion as he was returning home from court he was met by a little girl who wished to thank him for a judgement he had given in which a dog which had earlier been ordered to be destroyed was reprieved. The girl, a great dog lover, was delighted and as Lord Cooper was returning home she took the opportunity to tell him so. He was delighted to talk to her and brought her up to his study and explained to her the details of the case and how glad he was that it had given her pleasure. That little girl is now Lady Hope, the wife of the present Lord President of the Court of Session.

Although Lord Cooper signed my petition as an intrant to the Faculty of Advocates, remitting me for examination to the Dean and Faculty of Advocates, by the time I was called he had passed away so I never had the pleasure of appearing before him. The impression he left on my generation was of a patriotic Scotsman, a distinguished scholar, a balanced judge and a fine leader of the legal profession in Scotland.

The Saltire Society has in my view performed a valuable service to legal scholarship in re-publishing the first edition of Lord Cooper's influential essay, and accompanying it with two articles, by Professor Meston and Mr Sellar. Mr Sellar provides an erudite but eminently readable description of the historical background to Scots law and the Scottish legal system. Professor Meston provides a lucid and comprehensive description of modern Scots law and the modern Scottish legal system.

This work deserves to be read not only by Scots lawyers but by anyone interested in Scotland's distinctive history and institutions, and by lawyers from other traditions who see the value of the cross-fertilisation of legal tradition. Together, these three papers provide a fascinating portrait of Scotland's distinctive contribution to the legal heritage of the world.

LORD MACKAY OF CLASHFERN

Introduction

The original *Scottish Legal Tradition* is a unique work by a unique man, Lord Cooper, the only person this century to hold both of Scotland's senior judicial posts, having been first Justice-Clerk and then Lord President of the Court of Session. The Saltire Society was extremely fortunate to secure so distinguished a contributor, and ever since its publication in 1949 *The Scottish Legal Tradition* has been recognised as a classic. Written by one who sat at the very heart of the legal system every page of the work breathes the author's deep pride in and love of Scotland and her law. Lord Cooper was set an almost impossible brief, to write a survey of Scots law in little more than 12,000 words, but like the advocate he was, he more than rose to the challenge. *The Scottish Legal Tradition* managed to combine a concise survey of the long history of Scots law together with a review of the substantive law in a way that was both informative and entertaining.

With its elegant prose and inimitable style *The Scottish Legal Tradition* is a pleasure to read, and it has become the standard point of departure for anyone seeking an introduction to Scots law. Time moves on however and it became necessary to update Lord Cooper's work. This task was undertaken by Professor Meston of Aberdeen University and the Saltire Society was and is grateful to that author for his work in refurbishing *The Scottish Legal Tradition* for modern generations. However the changes in the law have grown ever larger and even in the field of legal history matters are not static. It is now generally recognised that Lord Cooper was mistaken on several historical points – in particular his thesis that after the Wars of Independence Scotland entered a 'legal Dark Age'. To incorporate these changes into Cooper's material would have required such major alterations that little would have remained of the original work. Rather than risk losing Lord Cooper's work altogether the Publications Committee of the Saltire Society, together with the Stair Society, decided to publish a completely new work under the now familiar collective title of *The Scottish Legal Tradition*.

This new *Scottish Legal Tradition* consists of two essays dealing respectively with the history and the present position of Scotland's legal tradition, together with a reprint of the first edition of Lord Cooper's original work (1949). The Societies are fortunate that two distinguished contemporary scholars agreed to write the new works. Professor Meston has provided a concise survey of those aspects of the contemporary substantive law previously covered by Lord Cooper; and David Sellar, a leading figure in the current renaissance of Scottish legal history, has written a fascinating overview of Scotland's legal history which will be an invaluable aid to anyone embarking on the study of this complex field. Lastly it was decided to invite Lord Dervaird to write a short Afterword on the future prospects of Scots law.

At the time of writing both the Scottish and English legal systems stand on the verge of immense changes, and the Saltire and Stair Societies are deeply honoured that the architect of these changes, Lord Mackay of Clashfern, the first Scots lawyer ever to sit on the Woolsack, so kindly agreed to provide the Foreword to this work.

It is in the nature of any collection such as this that the contributions should be very diverse but it is the hope of both Societies that in its own way this book may be seen as a continuation of the distinguished tradition established by Lord Cooper.

SCOTT CRICHTON STYLES
Old College,
University of Edinburgh,
May 1990

Scots Law Today

SCOTLAND'S PLACE IN THE INTERNATIONAL LEGAL ORDER

The constitutional structure of the United Kingdom causes considerable surprise to foreigners, for it does not readily fit any of the standard patterns. Even the name of the country causes confusion. The Frenchman who points out that he is Breton but also French cannot understand why the Scotsman refuses to accept that he is also English. The Netherlands suffer the same problem when we tend to call the country Holland, although that is only one of its parts. However, quite apart from the question of whether our country should be called England, Great Britain or the United Kingdom of Great Britain and Northern Ireland, there is often surprise at the degree of separation of its constituent parts.

The country is not a federation, but the parts retain a very high degree of separate identity. No other country plays international football and rugby as four separate national teams. It is a remarkable event when a single British Lions rugby team is from time to time selected to go on tour. Otherwise we see nothing peculiar in regarding matches between Scotland and England as internationals, and indeed if one refers to 'the' international, it is very likely to be taken as referring to the Scotland–England rugby match.

There is a single monarch, but the Royal Standard as flown in Scotland is different from that flown in England. The established church in England is entirely separate and different in nature from the established church in Scotland, and even the concept of 'establishment' differs sharply. Even public holidays differ. Scotland pays little attention to Easter holidays, and none at all to Whitsun, preferring to believe that Bank Holidays are intended as holidays for banks. Only recently has the Christmas period become a general public holiday in Scotland (in addition to the New Year) while England has begun to adopt the New Year in addition to Christmas.

The United Kingdom's diversity of structure stretches also to the legal field. When in 1707 separate Kingdoms of Scotland and England dissolved themselves and united into the new Kingdom of Great Britain, one of the important aspects of the Treaty concluded between the Kingdoms on 22 July 1706 and of the separate Acts of Union passed by the Parliaments of both Kingdoms, was the preservation of the separate identity of the Scottish legal system. There was little protection for the substance of the existing Scots law although laws concerning private right were not to be altered 'except for the evident utility of the subjects within Scotland'. However, the legal institutions, especially the Court of Session and the Court of Justiciary, were to remain in all time coming within Scotland.

The result now is that Scotland has laws, courts and legal professions quite separate from those of the other constituent parts of the United Kingdom. A lawyer qualified in England must retrain and requalify to become a Scottish legal practitioner and vice versa for a Scots lawyer in England. The Scottish criminal courts are final within Scotland, there being no appeal to the House of Lords from decisions made within Scotland. Although there is an appeal from decisions of the Court of Session on civil matters, the House of Lords applies Scots law (and not either English law or the non-existent U.K. law) in deciding a Scottish appeal.

David Sellar's elegant essay elsewhere in this book has explained the origins of the separate nature of the substantive law of Scotland. Although too much cannot and should not be made of the Romanist or Civilian nature of modern Scots law, there can be no doubt that the influence is there both in content and in methods of approaching problems. It is true that some of the apparent manifestations of Roman Law are not genuine. For example, the *legitim* of children and the *jus relictae* of a widow have their origin in Germanic customary law and have merely acquired Latinised titles. However, there is a civilian influence, which manifests itself in a less parochial approach to problems and a greater willingness to contemplate the solution derived from comparative study of other legal systems.

Modern life is based on much greater mobility of people and ideas. A greater internationalism is required, without losing the merits of existing systems. Every legal system, and especially those of small countries, must pay greater attention to what lawyers call private international law or conflict of laws to cope with situations where the laws of more than one country may be involved. When a cargo of wheat is shipped from the United States to France in a Dutch ship as a result of a contract made between a Spaniard and an Italian in Canada, many different systems, with different answers, might claim to be involved when something goes wrong.

Any small jurisdiction such as Scotland is likely to have these problems, and the growth of the oil industry in Scottish waters has meant that they are particularly acute. The oil industry employs so many people of diverse origins that conflicts between the various national legal systems arise on a regular basis—from the acceptability of driving licences to the recognition of marriages and divorces, or the proper formalities and content of wills. Major disasters such as the Piper Alpha platform explosion involve serious consideration of international elements of substantive law and of jurisdiction. Scotland has striven to take full account of these elements while carefully preserving what is best in its legal system.

The fierce independence of the Scots lawyer is not therefore based on parochial narrowness, but on a genuine recognition of the needs of the international community as well as of the merits which exist (along with defects!) in its own system. The fear is that a merger with English law would, through English ignorance, become a mere abolition of Scottish law and institutions. The gradual adoption of the better parts of Scots law in England demonstrates how the retention of a separate Scottish legal system has operated to the benefit of English law. Majority verdicts in criminal trials and a system of public prosecutors can be traced to Scottish practice. One can hope that reforms of the English house purchase practices will follow the Scottish pattern.

THE SCOTTISH COURTS AND THE LAW WHICH THEY APPLY

(a) *The Court Structure*
To understand the functions of the different hierarchies of courts it is necessary first to see the difference between civil and criminal law. While many laymen assume that a lawyer's life is largely concerned with the criminal law, this is true only of a very small proportion. Many highly successful lawyers will have little or no experience of criminal cases and they do not expect a steady flow of glamorous clients unjustly accused of murder. Criminal prosecutions are dealt with by one

hierarchy of courts—which are unfortunately always busy—while disputes over questions of civil law are decided in a different hierarchy.

It is not the nature of the actions by one of the parties which determines whether a case will be heard in the civil or in the criminal courts. A blow on the head may have both criminal and civil consequences. The assailant may be prosecuted for assault and be subjected to a criminal penalty but this does not end his civil liability to pay damages for the injury inflicted. The burglar can be sued in the civil courts both for the amount stolen and for the damage caused in breaking

CIVIL COURTS

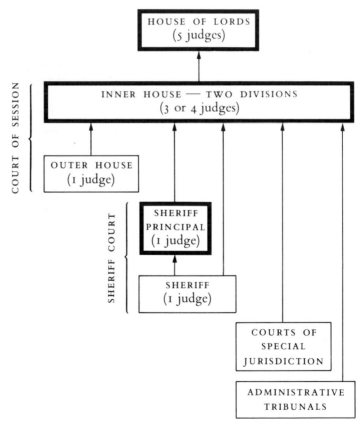

Note: HOUSE OF LORDS, INNER HOUSE and SHERIFF PRINCIPAL are Appellate Courts.

CRIMINAL COURTS

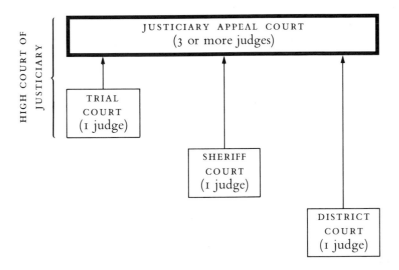

in. The reason why this is not more often done is the practical one that a convicted burglar is unlikely to have any assets from which the civil damages can be recovered. A court decree awarding a sum of money is not a cheque which can be cashed but merely permission to enforce it against any property which the defender may have. However to go some way to making recovery of damages easier for victims, criminal courts may now include compensation orders along with the criminal penalty.

In fact the difference between civil and criminal law boils down to one of the procedure adopted. Civil law is a facility which one citizen may use against another if he wishes to obtain a remedy. In criminal law the state takes action to apply a penalty for breach of the criminal law. Only in extremely rare cases is private prosecution still possible in Scotland, and even then any penalty is not for the benefit of the private prosecutor.

The courts with civil jurisdiction begin with the Sheriff Court. The origins of the office of sheriff are considered in the succeeding essay and here it is sufficient to say that Scotland is now split into six sheriffdoms, each presided over by a Sheriff Principal. Individual sheriff courts are distributed within the Sheriffdoms where the pressure of business requires. Several sheriffs may staff a busy court, while a single sheriff may deal with cases in a number of less busy courts.

The sheriff has very wide civil jurisdiction, recently made even wider. There is a simplified procedure for small claims and for summary causes involving up to £1500, but there is in general no upper limit to the value of a civil action which may be heard in the Sheriff Court. A small number of types of action may not be determined by a sheriff. These include declarators of nullity of marriage and special actions to set aside existing deeds or court decrees or to establish the true text of a lost document. However these exceptions may soon disappear and virtually every other category of litigation may be determined by a sheriff. Divorce, declarators of death and actions for very large awards of damages are all now common there.

Within Scotland, the highest civil court is the Court of Session which sits only in Edinburgh and does not go on circuit. In the Outer House (so named from the outer chamber of the old Tolbooth where the court once sat) fifteen judges sit singly in separate courts to hear cases raised for the first time before the Court of Session. Any civil case of any nature or value (other than cases for under £1500 which must go to the Sheriff Court) may be heard there.

Eight of the most senior judges form the Inner House of the Court, split into two Divisions. These are presided over by the Lord President and the Lord Justice-Clerk respectively and deal almost exclusively with appeals against decisions made in lower courts by sheriffs, sheriffs principal or Lords Ordinary in the Outer House. Novel cases may be heard by an enlarged court consisting in theory of up to the full complement of twenty-four judges; in practice the numbers are unlikely to exceed seven.

Most civil matters will be settled at this level but a further appeal does lie to the House of Lords, sitting in London, and perhaps a dozen cases a year from Scotland reach a final decision there. The House of Lords is also the final court of appeal from the English courts. In theory every one of the many hundreds of peers of the realm could sit on such an appeal but no lay peer has attempted to do so since 1883. In practice the legally qualified Lords of Appeal normally include two Scottish judges, who need not, however, necessarily be involved in Scottish appeals. The Lord Chancellor is the president of the court.

Outside the traditional structure a number of other courts have important functions in the civil sphere.

The Court of Justice of the European Communities—commonly known as the 'European Court'—sits in Luxembourg and has a growing influence as a result of its role in determining questions arising from the treaties, regulations and directives of various of the supra-national European institutions. Such determinations are binding on the national courts of member states.

A European institution which sits in Strasbourg and has caught the public imagination is the European Court of Human Rights. If a violation is alleged of a right protected by the European Convention on Human Rights the matter may end up in this court. However a complainer is often surprised to find that he cannot approach the Court directly and must take his case to the Commission on Human Rights hoping that it will investigate and see fit to raise the case before the court. A great many issues raise questions of human rights and ingenuity is finding more so that this tribunal is having a growing effect upon our law.

Within Scotland, it is possible to settle most civil disputes privately by appointing an arbiter (*anglicé*–arbitrator). The courts favour such settlements and will enforce awards properly made. In addition there are many other courts and tribunals of a specialised nature which deal with particular categories of dispute. Among them one may draw attention to the Scottish Land Court (dealing with matters of agricultural tenancies) and the related, but separate, Lands Tribunal for Scotland which deals with questions of the valuation of land and has, *inter alia*, the power to vary obligations in the title deeds of land. Very widely known is the network of Industrial Tribunals, whose best known function is to hear complaints and make awards in cases of unfair dismissal from employment. At the head of the network is the Employment Appeal Tribunal, with a further appeal to the Court of Session.

Finally in this brief selection of examples we must note the Lyon Court. It is presided over by the Lord Lyon, King of Arms and deals with all heraldic matters, including the grant of coats of arms, and in consequence, may settle questions of entitlement to the chieftainship of clans. As Lord Cooper notes, the court is by no means powerless, and the threat to send a man of skill—with his skilful axe—to 'ding doon' unauthorised coats of arms has had dramatic effects even upon government buildings.

The Scottish courts dealing with criminal matters begin with the District Court, the only example of a court composed entirely of lay judges in Scotland. First established in 1975, the court deals with minor criminal cases and despite its limited powers of sentence (60 days imprisonment or £1000 fine) it is being given a greater range of business. It is staffed by Justices of the Peace, who may sit singly, and is exclusively a court of summary procedure.

The Sheriff Court also has a function in hearing criminal cases, under both summary and solemn procedure, and in fact deals with the majority of all the criminal cases in Scotland. Powers of sentence vary according to the procedure adopted, but can include imprisonment for up to three years and an unlimited fine. Virtually any criminal offence can be dealt with by the sheriff, apart from the exclusive jurisdiction of the High Court of Justiciary.

The members of the High Court are the same judges who are also the judges of the court of Session in civil cases but in the High Court, the Lord President assumes the title of Lord Justice-General. The High Court is the supreme criminal court for Scots law and has exclusive jurisdiction in certain very serious crimes such as treason, murder and rape. Other prosecutions of a type which might competently be heard in lower courts may in fact be heard by a single judge of the High Court (with a jury) if particularly serious or if it seems likely that the penalty which would be imposed on conviction would be beyond the powers of a sheriff.

Appeal from decisions at first instance in any of these criminal courts lies to the High Court sitting as the Court of Criminal Appeal. This consists normally of three senior judges of the High Court and its decision is final. In distinction from civil matters, there is no appeal to the House of Lords on matters of Scottish criminal law.

(b) *Sources of Law*
Legislation. It is a normal and natural aspiration of human nature that all material relevant to a particular activity should be available in one place. In the context of legal rules, this demand has led to the preparation of great codes of law in which both broad principle and some detailed application of the principle can be found in a single volume. The Emperor Justinian in the 6th Century instigated the creation of such a compilation, and much of continental Europe followed suit more than 1000 years later, sometimes exporting their codes to countries such as Japan. Although everyone seems to have heard of the *Code Napoléon*, the influence of the French Emperor Napoleon was in truth no more

than to give an impetus to a process already under way with the editing and publishing of the previous compilations of customary law in various parts of France. The *Coutume de Paris* can be traced at many points in the Napoleonic Code. Scotland began to follow the same path when Viscount Stair's *Institutions* (1681) systematised the previous amalgam of disparate rules of law in Scotland. However, Scotland never reached the point of a fully fledged code of law and our sources remain multiple and of varying importance. In part this is inevitable, for even those legal systems which have codified their law and which formally prohibit the use of any other sources of law (e.g. France) do find in practice that other sources have to be drawn upon. Judicial decisions are in fact heavily relied upon in France, even if theoretically only as illustrations of how a text has been construed in the past, and the actual, as opposed to the theoretical, result is that even in a codified system, many different sources have to be consulted to establish what the law is.

In Scotland, the primary source of law today is clearly legislation of one type or another. This view was not held even fifty years ago, when legislation could be regarded as an occasional (and usually faulty) excrescence upon the main body of the law. However the primacy of formal legislative enactment cannot now be denied. Statutes of the U.K. Parliament can override all other sources of law, except fundamental constitutional provisions and European law, and the very rare cases involving rules of morality of so fundamental a nature that they count as superior natural law. There are very few of these, if indeed any exist at all, but a case in point may be a court's authority to ignore the precise and unambiguous terms of the statute regulating inheritance when the beneficiary under the statute has murdered the person whose estate is being inherited. The murderer is in fact treated as disqualified from inheriting by virtue of a rule mostly dependent upon common law, but the precise and unqualified statute has to be ignored to achieve that result. It is beneficial that it should be ignored, but this very special case may indicate that legislation can sometimes be at least modified by higher, non-statutory, values.

However, apart from these special cases, it is clear that the output of Parliament and other bodies with legislative powers is now both the most important source of law and the commonest source of law. Legal training more and more involves detailed analysis of the exact text of a legislative enactment and attempts to assess its meaning in various potential applications. In most situations in which one tries to establish what the law is, one now looks first for statutory provisions. As indicated in the following essay, the past thirty years have seen very substantial statutory enactments in areas formerly governed only by case law, and even if the Scottish flavour is preserved, the nature of the lawyer's task has changed.

Legislation comes in many forms. As already noted, some of it still consists of the statutes passed by the Scots Parliament before 1707. Unlike modern legislation this has the characteristic of extreme brevity, but what it lacks in detailed exposition it gains in pungency. Who could fail to understand the Act of 1597 (*c.* 3) 'Kirkyard dykes should be biggit' or fail to applaud the sentiment of the Act of 1482 (*c.* 7)—now repealed—that 'no person within the realm shall mix wine or beer under the pain of death'?

The post-1707 legislation of the United Kingdom Parliament has become steadily lengthier, more complex and wider in the aims which it hopes to achieve as time has gone by. While some of it may come close to the limit of what law can achieve, techniques of legislative drafting have made it possible to regulate successfully areas of law previously felt to be unsuitable for statute. It is clearly essential to have precise legislative enactment in areas, especially of commercial law, where detailed regulation of the running of companies and of solicitations for investment are needed to provide security and confidence for business transactions. Hence the massive size of the Companies Acts and the Financial Services Act 1986, while the need for precision in tax matters leads to nearly 1500 pages of the Income and Corporation Taxes Act 1988.

Much legislative detail now is contained in delegated legislation. Parliament can authorise individuals such as Secretaries of State or the Registrar General to make orders or regulations within particular limits, and orders or statutory instruments issued under these powers have the full force of a statute enacted by Parliament itself. In any given year the volume of delegated legislation on such matters as the Road Traffic Construction and Use Regulations is many times greater than the output of statutes from Parliament itself. The practical problem of finding all such delegated legislation on a particular problem can be large, and even Parliament has difficulty in devising means of keeping adequate control of it, but no other method yet exists for making the kind of detailed provision which seems nowadays to be necessary.

The main remaining type of legislation is one which has been of growing importance since Britain's accession to the European Community. The European Communities Act 1972 directs British courts to give effect to all enforceable rights and obligations arising under the treaties setting up the European Communities. The result is that Community Regulations are immediately and directly part of our law as if they were U.K. statutes. Community Directives direct member states to achieve a given result by a given date, but leave it up to the member states to use the methods appropriate to their legal systems. In limited circumstances, and once the deadline has passed, even a Directive may be treated as if it were a statute in the sense of conferring rights on individuals who would have benefited if the Directive had been implemented. Normally however a Directive is an instruction to a government and not a rule of law for a court to apply.

Precedent. The second main source to which a lawyer looks for the law dealing with a particular problem is the law derived from previous decisions. These decisions—the 'common law'—produce rules of law and not merely illustrations of the application of the law. A graphic demonstration of this is a comment by Megarry, J. in an English case on a point which had not arisen before. In giving his decision, he said, 'It may be that there is no direct authority on this point—certainly none has been cited. If so, it is high time that there was such authority, and now there is.'

Many criticisms can be made of the use of 'judge-made law'. A judge is not responsible to an electorate, and his decision in the first case of a particular type is in reality retrospective legislation. However the consistency of decision in similar cases which is promoted by the use of past cases as precedents is an important element of justice and in the result it is clear that precedent must be a source of law.

It is not necessary for this that a single precedent should be binding on all future courts, but England and, it would seem, Scotland have adopted a strict version of the doctrine of *stare decisis* under which a single decision from a qualifying court will bind all future courts dealing with the same point of law. In very broad terms, subject to particular qualifications, a decision of a superior court binds lower courts to follow that decision. At one time the House of Lords regarded itself as bound to follow its own previous decisions (with the result that legislation was needed to reverse them) but is now prepared to ignore its own previous decisions in the rare cases where this is necessary (as in *Dick* v *Burgh of*

Falkirk in 1976 where a contrary decision made in 1892 was expressly overruled because it would now have produced injustice to a litigant). Whatever the relative status of the courts involved, it is only when the same point of law is being considered that the later court can be bound by the earlier. There is much scope for debate about what was the real point of law (what lawyers call the *ratio decidendi*) in the first case. Many of the potentially harsh effects of strictly following a single precedent are in practice avoided by careful examination of what was necessary for a decision in the previous case. Only what was actually and necessarily decided in one case can be binding in the future. That may not be easy to establish. In the celebrated case of *Donoghue* v *Stevenson* in 1932 a decision was reached on the assumption that a decomposing snail did float out of a ginger-beer bottle in a café in Paisley, causing harm to Mrs Donoghue who had been drinking some of the ginger beer earlier. Was the point of law necessarily decided by the House of Lords the very broad principle that everyone must take reasonable steps to avoid injuring persons who might reasonably be considered likely to be affected by his actions? Alternatively was it that manufacturers of Scottish ginger beer in opaque bottles must take reasonable care to prevent snails getting into bottles intended to be sold in Paisley cafés? In practice the *ratio decidendi* has come to be much nearer the first of these as it has been applied in very many subsequent cases. A dinner (with snails) was recently held to celebrate this landmark case.

Minor sources. Other sources of law are much less important in terms of the number of occasions on which they are invoked, but may be very significant when new issues have to be decided.

Legal writing does not in general qualify as an authoritative source of law in the sense that a judge may be bound to follow the author's view. Weight and respect may be given to the work depending on the force of the reasoning and the author's reputation, but it is the court which makes the authoritative decision. However, in Scotland there are certain 'Institutional' writings, which have force as sources of actual law to be applied by the courts and not merely adopted or rejected. There is no final and definitive list of works entitled to this institutional status, but in civil (as opposed to criminal) law, it certainly includes Stair's *Institutions* (1681), Bankton's *Institute* (1751), Erskine's *Institute* (1773) and Bell's *Commentaries* (1800/1804) and probably also Kames's *Principles of Equity* (1760). The classic works accorded institutional status fit uneasily into a system based on the primacy of legislation and judicial decision, but clearly have the attribute of being law rather than merely about law.

Rarely will the courts have to go beyond these three sources— legislation, precedent and institutional writings—for their law, but it may be necessary to fall back upon the custom of those involved in a particular trade or living in a particular locality. If custom is invoked it will normally be as a local exception to the general rule, and it is particularly important in establishing public rights of way over privately owned land.

A court is not permitted to turn litigants away on the ground that there are no rules of law about the matter in dispute. It must reach a decision, and if all else fails, general principles of equity and reason may have to be called upon, aided by any examples of decisions in other countries where the same problem has been addressed.

THE LAW OF OBLIGATIONS

It is of the essence of law that it enforces minimum standards and not desirable aspirations. It can stop me by interdict from doing something which clearly goes beyond the bounds of conduct tolerable by most of society. Driving at 100 mph while drunk clearly offends against several minimum standards set by society and would subject me to penalties in the criminal courts. If I have made a contract I can be forced to carry it out exactly according to the terms, or to pay damages for the loss caused.

What law cannot do is to make me act enthusiastically, or to go beyond the strict letter of my legal obligation. A sense of fairness and equity might well suggest that I should do more, or that what I do in fact may not be within the spirit of the agreement though just within its letter. In a memorable phrase, the nineteenth-century Scottish judge, Lord Neaves, described this as 'keeping the wind of the law'. Using a very broad brush one can say that the law cannot force me to be good, it can only prevent me from being too bad. This may be why the Christian golden rule 'do unto others as you would wish them to do unto you' is an exhortation and could not be a law. A legally enforceable version of the same rule would have to start from the negative command, 'do *not* unto others what you would not wish them to do unto you'.

Obligations of the type which the law can enforce are the very stuff of any legal system. The law is there to set out what these enforceable obligations are and to provide the means of enforcing them if they are not obeyed. In Scotland, as in any other system, the law of obligations is divided into two branches of law: the law of contract and the law of delict. Very large and extensive books are written on both topics, but in broad terms the law of contract concerns the making, interpretation, application and enforcement of contracts or binding agreements. The law of delict (better known in Anglo-American legal circles as the law of tort) concerns the situations in which harm is caused to one person by another in such circumstances that the latter must compensate his victim.

The fundamental approach of the Scots law of contract is that it enforces promises rather than bargains. Of course the promises must have been seriously intended as commitments and it must be possible to prove that they have been made, but it is the promise which is enforced. It is not essential that the beneficiary of the promise should give anything, even a counter-promise, in return, so that it is not the element of bargain which makes agreements binding. This means, in legal parlance, that Scotland does not have the requirement of 'consideration' which is such an important feature of the English law of contract.

It is true that in practical terms this does not often lead to differences in the result which the systems reach. English law has been ingenious in finding consideration in many situations which Scotland would classify as unilateral and gratuitous, with the consequence that seriously intended commitments are usually binding in both systems. The one situation in which a clear difference can be seen arises when the seller of a house offers to sell at a particular price and then gratuitously agrees to keep the offer open for a week. That unilateral promise to keep the offer open is binding in Scotland—provided its existence can be proved to the stiffer than normal standard required. It would not be binding in England.

Contracts arise in a huge range of circumstances and are not necessarily as formal as many people think. It is not necessary that there should be a large document with seals, signatures and 'heretofores' and 'whereases'. Indeed writing is very rarely necessary at all, and legal gobbledegook certainly is not necessary. We make contracts every day by handing over money for a coffee, by filling a car's petrol tank at a self-service pump, or by buying a train ticket. We may make a contract of loan with a building society or bank or act as guarantor for someone else's loan. The contract may involve twenty pence for a newspaper or twenty million pounds for a piece of oilfield equipment. The circumstances are infinitely various, but all have the feature that some words, writing or actions constitute an offer by one person and similar words, writing or actions are deemed to be an acceptance by the other person. From the moment of acceptance (which may be when a letter of acceptance is dropped into the post box) the agreement exists and both are committed. In 1891, when Mrs Carlill bought her smoke ball in reliance on an advertisement placed by the Carbolic Smoke Ball Company and acted upon the instructions in the advertisement there existed a contract including the terms set out in the advertisement. To the company's horror, it found that it was liable to pay her the reward it had promised in the advertisement when she caught flu. Advertisements are rarely so precise now.

It is not even necessary in Scotland that only the two parties to the contract can enforce it. If a contract is made between A and B for the benefit of C, Scots law does recognise the possibility that C can enforce the contract directly as a result of what we call a *jus quaesitum tertio*.

While parties are normally free to make their own agreements, this can lead to the party with greater economic strength being able to dictate terms to the other on a 'take it or leave it' basis. Abuse of that power by inserting unfair conditions in the small print of large documents has in recent years led to legislation to protect the consumer. Hence it is no longer possible for finance companies to save themselves the bother of having to sue a defaulting debtor in the courts of his home town by inserting a clause entitling them to sue in a court convenient to them which he may not be able to afford to attend. One doubts whether many who used to sign agreements knew what 'prorogating the jurisdiction of the Sheriff Court in Glasgow' meant. More recently, the Unfair Contract Terms Act 1977 has sharply reduced the ability of businesses to restrict the amount of their liability in the event of their own breach of their contract. They can no longer exclude their liability to a purchaser injured by the explosion of an electrical appliance under the guise of a 'guarantee' to replace the appliance. A high pressure insurance salesman, skilled in the art of 'closing' a sale, now finds that the Insurance Companies Act 1982 gives his victim a 'cooling off' period in which to withdraw.

If there is a breach of contract, the courts exist to give a means of redress if required. In theory, the primary right of the pursuer (not 'plaintiff' in Scotland) is that his contract should be carried out. Hence in theory the main remedy is that of 'specific implement' ordering the defender to do what he has contracted to do—be that building a wall, buying a house, constructing an oil platform, or singing at a concert. However enforced performance is rarely good performance and in many situations the effect of the breach is that performance is no longer possible. In practice therefore the normal remedy is a court award of a sum of money as damages, the pursuer then being free to collect that sum from the person in breach—if any funds exist!

The law of delict concerns the other great branch of the obligations which may be incurred. If by my negligent actions I cause harm or injury to anyone to whom I owe a duty of care, I can be required to compensate the injured party. The subject is a vast one, and much subtle analysis goes into questions of 'fault' or 'negligence' or 'duty of care'. Indeed in some situations there is strict liability without need to prove any fault, usually when some inherently hazardous occupation is being carried on.

Actions will normally be brought directly against the person causing the harm and thus in Mrs Donoghue's celebrated action arising out of the snail in her ginger-beer bottle, she sought damages from the manufacturer who permitted snails to get into his bottle store. For the good reason that employers are on average more likely to be able to pay damages than is the average employee, action will normally be taken against the employer as vicariously liable for the actions of his employee in the course of his employment. Much subtle argument can be devoted to the apparently innocent phrase 'in the course of his employment'.

Common examples of delictual actions which come before the courts are for the cost of repairs to motor vehicles damaged in collisions and, especially, actions for damages for personal injuries. Very large sums are necessary to compensate—to the extent that money can compensate—for severe incapacitating injury; and such sums are being awarded. But the fundamental rule that compensation can be awarded only when the defender can be proved to have been at fault does lead to hardship when fault cannot be proved, and there is growing pressure to establish a 'no-fault' compensation system. Such a system postulates some kind of national fund to make the payments, for from the point of view of the person shown *not* to have been at fault, it is grossly unfair that he should have to pay damages. The injured person, on the other hand, has a legitimate interest in obtaining an award of money—without undue delay or difficulty—to enable him to adapt to his new situation. It seems very probable that some version of a no-fault scheme will in the foreseeable future be enacted.

Whether or not such a scheme does come about, the size of awards of damages is certain to continue to be a matter of considerable public interest. The Piper Alpha tragedy in 1988 in which a large number of men lost their lives in a huge explosion and fire on an oil platform has again brought attention to bear upon the problem.

What is not always realised is that damages are intended to compensate the pursuer for the loss which that pursuer has sustained, and are not penalties imposed on the person causing the harm. Scots law does not have the concept of penal damages over and above the actual loss suffered, and although a penalty payable to the State may be appropriate in criminal proceedings, it is difficult to see why a victim should get twice as much as a proper award of compensation to mark displeasure at the defender who caused the harm. The consequence of the purely compensatory nature of our awards of damages is that very different sums can be awarded to different pursuers, depending on future prospects and the number of dependants.

There is strong pressure to bring Scottish ideas of what is a proper award of compensation closer to the level of awards in the United States of America. Out of court settlements in cases where the possibility exists of action in the U.S. courts are now being based on what is commonly called a 'Mid-Atlantic' formula and no doubt the influence of reports of such awards will tend to increase the sums claimed and awarded in Scotland.

Another problem of great debate is how the injured person can afford the cost of the necessary litigation. Scotland has a long and proud tradition of legal aid voluntarily provided by the legal profession since 1424. In the present century a statutory scheme has provided assistance for the poor in civil cases, and the scheme has been extended to criminal cases and to advice about possible legal claims. However the qualifying income is set at a very low level, considerable delays can occur before legal aid is granted and the claim, not unreasonably, must pass a test of probability of success. Those not far above the qualifying income limit can feel that the risk of paying the expenses of both parties if the claim fails is too great to justify proceeding with a claim. There is therefore some suggestion that lawyers should charge fees only in the event of being successful.

It is already possible in Scotland (though not apparently in England) for a court lawyer to make an agreement with his client for payment only in the event of success. In that event, the payment would be only at the normal rates, with no allowance for the risk that the work involved would be wholly unremunerated, and it is not perhaps surprising that such agreements are relatively rare. However, it is a method by which, if there is agreement, a client may insulate himself from part of the potential costs if a court action fails.

There would probably be little resistance to a proposal that in such speculative actions the normal fee might be assessed at a rather higher rate to reflect the risk undertaken by the lawyer, but very strong passions are aroused when there are suggestions for American-style 'contingency fees'. Under this system, lawyers can contract with clients for a fee expressed as, say, one third or even one half, of any damages recovered for the client. Obviously such a fee can be paid only in the event of success. As the United States does not in general apply the rule that the loser pays the expenses of both sides, the result is that a client making a claim for damages can be insulated from all risk, but at the expense of losing a substantial proportion of the award designed to compensate him. This can be seen as a safe method of enabling the poorer client to press a justifiable claim, but it also means that the lawyer has a personal interest in the outcome of the litigation he is conducting for his client. The result in the U.S.A. is that awards of damages by juries can be higher than required for compensation, if jurors add a percentage to ensure that the 'correct' sum is left after the lawyer's fee has been deducted. It is to be hoped that Scotland never abandons the proud tradition of independence of the legal profession by giving the lawyer part ownership of the subject of litigation.

FAMILY LAW

For a long time the family law of Scotland was based almost entirely on the common law with very little statutory intervention. Even the existence of divorce for adultery depended only upon judicial decisions from the time of the Reformation in 1560 until it first was statutorily enacted as a ground of divorce by the Divorce (Scotland) Act 1976.

Many other features of Scottish family law remained as they had been from time immemorial—which was no doubt a comfort to veteran lawyers who did not have to relearn their law! However society has changed greatly over the past 50 years and expectations have changed radically. The result has been a great deal of legislation affecting parts of family life which would previously have been regarded as outwith the scope of legal regulation. While Lord Cooper could in his original classic pamphlet regard the statutory introduction of adoption as 'an anomalous inroad upon the common law' the merits or demerits of which were open to question, the flow of statutes has been such that very little indeed of the common law is still in force. In general the quality of the statutes has been high, although some of them, such as the Matrimonial Homes (Family Protection) (Scotland) Act 1981, have created many difficulties in their practical application.

In view of the comprehensive coverage of recent legislation which has been the subject of wide consultation the opportunity exists for the preparation of a true code of family law for Scotland. Such a code, consolidating the diverse existing statutes and setting out the whole law in a rational manner would be a welcome development of Scots law. Already the Family Law (Scotland) Act 1985 c. 37 provides the basis of a code of law regulating matrimonial property and aliment.

Scotland used to be famous (or notorious) for its forms of irregular marriage, the origins of which are explained by David Sellar elsewhere in this volume. At Gretna Green and Coldstream, both places where the Scottish border is easily identifiable by natural features, a marriage industry developed where semi-professional witnesses heard the declarations of marriage made by couples fleeing from parental wrath in England. Oddly enough, there is severe doubt whether a blacksmith was involved during the heyday of irregular marriage before a residential requirement was imposed in 1856. The only remaining irregular marriage is now by cohabitation with habit and repute—defined by Lord Neaves as 'living a good while together and getting a married repute'. This gives the protection of genuine married status in situations where no formal ceremony has occurred. It must be distinguished from the position of the woman referred to in the Press as a 'common law wife' when what is meant is a cohabitee who is *not* married. An irregular marriage is fully recognised for all purposes and can be terminated only by divorce.

There is, however, a growing recognition of the position of the cohabitee for a number of specific, and very limited, purposes. For example an established cohabitee is entitled to apply to a court for an order granting occupancy rights in the home under the Matrimonial Homes (Family Protection) (Scotland) Act 1981, but only for six months at a time. Reform of the law of succession to the estate of a deceased person may include some provision for the cohabitee, and cohabitation is already equated with marriage for many purposes within the social security legislation.

Marriage alters very many legal relationships, but one aspect which causes interest is the name which a married woman may or must use. The normal Scottish practice is that on marriage a woman adopts her husband's surname and becomes for example Mrs Smith. Sometimes by excess of zeal she will be referred to by his christian name as well, e.g. Mrs John Smith. In formal legal documents the practice is to add the husband's surname to her own (e.g. Mrs Mary Jones or Smith) and this has the great merit of assisting identification by indicating both maiden and married names. However all this is in fact no more than practice based on undoubted convenience. It is not essential that a married woman takes her husband's surname and it has not always been the Scottish tradition that she should do so; indeed until the 18th century wives rarely took their husbands' names. The practice seems to have been imported from England.

Divorce has been part of the law of Scotland since the Reformation, both adultery and desertion having been grounds of divorce since the 16th century. It was originally envisaged as a penalty on a spouse guilty of one of these serious matrimonial offences, but the trend in the 20th century has been away from the matrimonial offence theory to a recognition of the reality of breakdown of a relationship. Indeed since the Divorce (Scotland) Act 1976, breakdown of marriage has been in theory the only ground of divorce, but the only method of proving breakdown is to establish one of five grounds. Three of these, adultery, intolerable behaviour and desertion, are fault based and two avoid questions of fault by being based on de facto separation for two or five years, depending upon the defender's consent. The non-fault separation grounds now account for approximately half of all divorces and it may be that reform will bring a single ground of divorce based on separation for a short period, or even on mere lapse of time after one party gives notice of intention to divorce. It is probably fruitless to debate whether easier divorce is a cause or a result of more frequent breakdowns of marriages, but there is no evidence that more difficult conditions for divorce would reduce the number of broken marriages. The aim of the law must be, in the light of the changing patterns of society at a given time, to permit dead marriages to be buried without creating new and unnecessary hostility.

Matrimonial property is another area in which radical and welcome change has brought greater justice into our law. Until very recently it was possible to say that the only two faults with the Scottish matrimonial property system were that there was no matrimonial property and no system. Each spouse owned what he or she brought to the marriage and any property or savings derived from their separate earnings. Marriage had virtually no consequences upon property except upon death or divorce, when limited special rights existed.

Rights of inheritance by a surviving spouse were substantially improved in 1964 and seem likely to be still further improved in a forthcoming comprehensive statute on the law of succession. Property settlements on divorce were also improved in 1964 but have since been further amended culminating in the very important Family Law (Scotland) Act 1985. That Act sets out a general principle on divorce that property acquired during the marriage other than windfalls to one spouse by gift or inheritance should be shared equally between the spouses. That property includes what is often the main asset, namely accrued pension rights. While this is in form a prescription for settlement on divorce only, there can be little doubt that this recognises and encourages the common practice in the normal stable marriage of treating assets as a common pool available to both spouses. However the only express provision for property relations during the subsistence of marriage is that household goods and any savings from a housekeeping allowance are shared equally.

The position of children has also been the subject of major changes in recent years. Foremost among the changes which have improved social justice is the abolition—so far as any law can have that effect—of the status of illegitimacy. Apart from the special case of titles of honour and coats of arms, the Law Reform (Parent and Child) (Scotland) Act 1986 made the marriage or lack of marriage of its parents irrelevant to the legal status of a child. It is to be hoped that Scottish society will simply cease to use the term 'illegitimate' now that this radical reform has come into force.

Equally it is to be hoped that parents in dispute will cease to use the

21

child as a weapon against each other, and to this end the Child Abduction and Custody Act 1985 has taken a valuable, if small, step to reduce the number of international 'snatches' of children in custody disputes.

One traditional feature of Scots law relating to children which still remains is the much greater capacity to enter into contracts than in the case of English children. For both countries the age of full legal capacity—'majority'—has been reduced to 18, but in Scotland when a child attains the age of 12, if a girl, and 14, if a boy, it becomes a 'minor' and has very substantial powers to make binding contracts. While seriously disadvantageous contracts made by a minor can be set aside by the courts during the *quadriennium utile*, or the four years after majority, many are surprised to find that a minor has the power to make a valid will, irrespective of consent by a guardian.

A feature of the Scottish law affecting children which is the subject of international praise is the system of Children's Hearings set up by the Social Work (Scotland) Act 1968. At such hearings a panel of lay persons decides whether children brought before them are in need of compulsory measures of care such as supervision requirements. The reason for referral may be commission of an offence by the child or it may be commission of an offence against the child or other reason why care and supervision are required. In any of these situations the hearing is primarily concerned with the welfare of the child and does not determine questions of guilt or innocence or any disputed question of fact.

THE LAW OF PROPERTY

The word 'property' is used in different senses, but for our purpose it denotes the assets of any kind which an individual may own and is not restricted to land and houses. Scotland still draws a distinction between heritable property and moveable property similar to that between real and personal property in the English system. Heritable property, in broad terms, consists of land and things attached to it on a permanent basis while moveable property includes everything else. It is not necessarily clear that the distinction still serves a useful purpose and heritage is certainly much less significant than formerly as the main element of wealth.

Scottish land law is one of the areas of undisturbed indigenous growth over centuries and it is quite distinct from the separately developed system in England. The Scots law draws its fundamental doctrines from a pure form of feudal theory, and this is the source of its great strengths—despite the fact that the word 'feudal' has come to be a term of abuse.

As Lord Cooper says in his original pamphlet, 'In the seventeenth and eighteenth centuries and even earlier, our classical system of conveyancing and heritable rights was worked out to the last detail with a rigorous logic and a felicitous ingenuity which it is a pleasure to study.' The logic, which is still present in our conveyancing system, resulted in a careful process of connecting the title of one owner to that of the last, and especially upon the public registration of all deeds affecting land in the Register of Sasines. The principle of 'the faith of the records' meant that reliance could be placed on the Register (and some related Registers) to give information about any deeds affecting land. As very few interests in land can be created without a deed (primarily rights of way and, recently, a spouse's occupancy rights in a matrimonial home) a high level of security of title can be achieved. Title insurance is virtually unknown, because it is unnecessary, and even the most meticulous and pedantic of conveyancers can usually be satisfied from the records that his client will receive a good title. Law students tend to grumble about the antiquity and complexity of the system, but when they become qualified lawyers they see the huge merits of security for their clients.

However it is true that the security has been bought at the expense of a degree of complexity not always acceptable today. The Register of Sasines is a register of deeds with the result that every deed must be examined on every transfer. Improvements are under way in a slow (indeed unduly slow) process of transferring all landownership in Scotland to a system of registration of title rather than of deeds. Under this system the deeds making up the title are fully investigated once and for all and, once registered, the title is guaranteed by the state. Whether this system will, as Lord Cooper predicted, produce transfers of land at 'trifling' cost remains to be seen, but the system is certainly cheaper and simpler, while preserving the great merits of the Scottish tradition.

One of the features of the Scottish pattern of houseownership which causes some surprise to the English lawyer is the easy acceptance of the concept of individual ownership of flats in a tall tenement building. Indeed Edinburgh can almost be said to have had the first skyscrapers as the tall buildings surrounding Parliament Square in the eighteenth century reached about 130 feet in height. Each flat is capable of being owned outright without involving any formal joint venture by means of a company or condominium. The common law implies the necessary rights of support and enforceable common interest with the others in the roof and foundations.

The other aspect of Scottish practice which has recently aroused much comment is the house purchase system. A potential purchaser can, and does, have his surveys and other investigations completed before making his offer. The offer is not therefore a mere declaration of interest, and acceptance of the offer by the seller immediately creates a binding contract. There is no scope for gazumping either by the seller accepting a later and higher offer or by the purchaser choosing to buy another house. The English practice of obtaining a deposit (which is of questionable value even there) has normally no place in a Scottish sale and finality is achieved at an early stage. Only the growing practice of having extremely detailed offers and acceptances ('the missives') may threaten the valued speed and finality.

The feudal system is being reformed by prohibition of the creation of new feuduties (payments to feudal superiors) and compulsory redemption of existing feuduties on a sale. The whole system may eventually be abolished by cancellation of the remaining legal relationship between superior and vassal. However, although the resulting system would be new, it would still be based on the solid foundations established by the great feudalists of the past.

Inheritance of property is one of the most fertile sources of family arguments, although these arguments less frequently reach the stage of court litigation than once was the case. When the deceased person has not made a will, the law which has been in force since 1964 has done a great deal to bring the law into line with modern expectations. No longer does the eldest son inherit all the land. No longer is a spouse treated as an inferior dependant. No longer are maternal relatives excluded. No longer is the illegitimate child ignored. The spouse's 'prior right' gives him or her the whole of the deceased's intestate estate unless the estate is substantial. Further reform is promised to remove technical flaws in the law and to reinforce the primacy of the position of the surviving spouse. This is likely to mean that most children will have no share in a parent's estate if the other parent is still alive, a result which would agree with the normal expectations of Scots.

When we turn to wills, however, there have been fewer statutory variations upon the common law. A formal will is signed before two witnesses, but Scotland takes a liberal approach to the making of wills and also accepts the 'holograph' will written and signed wholly in the testator's handwriting. Such a will does not require witnesses, so that even a pencil note on the back of an envelope can suffice if it is signed and is clearly meant to be a will.

The freedom to make a will without advice does of course sometimes lead to problems of interpretation of the words used, and it is too late to ask the testator. What, for example, does one make of a will which leaves one half to X, one quarter to Y and the remaining 'third' to Z? None the less, the freedom to use the unwitnessed holograph will has been very valuable in giving effect to genuine expressions of intention, and it is possible that the courts may be given power to ignore any defects in formalities if a document is clearly genuine.

Many doctrines have been developed to limit the enthusiasm of testators with inflated ideas of their power. Money cannot simply be left to grow over extended periods, nor can a testator try to control the lives of generations yet to come. Working rules of interpretation cover common contingencies like the birth of a child after a will has been made or the birth of children to a legatee who has predeceased. Statute now tells us how to cope with the common calamity in which two people die together (apart from spouses the younger survives the elder) and also what to do when someone simply disappears.

One of the most distinctive features of Scots inheritance law has for a long time been the 'legal rights' of spouses and children. These rights are probably the remnant of a system under which the family as a whole owned property, but now take the form of guaranteed rights to fixed fractions of the property of the deceased parent or spouse. They cannot be defeated by anything in the deceased's will and hence give protection against disinheritance. The fixed share system has the great merit of predictability, simplicity and cheapness, and it is unlikely that Scotland will follow the pattern set by New Zealand and England of giving a discretion to the court to make such awards as it thinks fit.

CRIMINAL LAW AND PROCEDURE

The law and procedure relating to crime are parts of the legal system with a particularly Scottish flavour. They are parts of which Scotland can justifiably feel proud, for they have developed through experience and have proved eminently capable of meeting changed requirements. It is a subject of debate whether the High Court of Justiciary has power to declare new crimes, but there is no doubt that the Court has done Scotland a service by dealing with new ways of committing old crimes. The High Court was able to respond to the age of the motor car by finding the taking away of cars to be criminal well before Parliament enacted legislation. Recently it has been widely applauded for establishing that selling glue-sniffing kits to children is criminal at common law, without the need for Parliament to enact a statute on the point.

Very substantial protection for an accused person is built into Scottish criminal procedure, and several editors of national newspapers have found to their cost that publication of photographs of an accused before trial is treated as a serious contempt of court. There is no preliminary hearing in public and at the trial there is no opening statement by the prosecution of what it thinks it can prove. What is actually proved emerges from the evidence and the defence always has the last word in a trial. Alleged confessions by the accused are admitted relatively rarely and then under safeguards to ensure that they are genuine. All substantial points in the prosecution case require to be corroborated through the evidence of more than one witness. The necessary corroboration does not necessarily require that two eye-witnesses be present, but the requirement does mean that, apart from some statutory offences, no one can be convicted on the evidence of a single witness, however credible.

The decision on whether to prosecute and, if so, for what crime is, for practical purposes, exclusively in the hands of the public prosecution service. The Lord Advocate is at the head of the service and acts through Advocates-Depute in the Crown Office and the procurators fiscal in each sheriff and district court. Private prosecution is possible in some very rare circumstances and was indeed adopted only a few years ago when technical reasons prevented public prosecution in the notorious Glasgow rape case. However the previous occasion on which private prosecution occurred was in 1909 and one can reasonably say that it is a very unusual exception to the rule. There is no question of the police prosecuting in Scotland, their duty being to report facts to the procurator fiscal for his decision and to take instructions from him for investigations into crime.

The public prosecutor has complete control of the proceedings. It is for the Lord Advocate or Procurator Fiscal to decide whether an offence is of sufficient gravity to justify the use of solemn procedure—in which case a jury of 15 persons will decide upon guilt or innocence—or whether a summary prosecution will suffice. If the decision is for summary procedure a justice of the peace or sheriff sitting without a jury will determine both guilt and the sentence to be imposed if the accused is found guilty. The accused does not have a right to insist upon jury trial, and rarely suggests it in view of the increased powers of sentence of a sheriff under solemn procedure. The wide discretion conferred upon the Crown in the conduct of prosecutions is justified by the long and honourable tradition of impartiality and fairness in the conduct of a prosecution, and extends to the point that if the prosecutor does not move for sentence, even after a finding of guilt, the court has no power to impose a sentence.

There is no appeal to the House of Lords in criminal matters so that criminal cases begin and end within the Scottish legal system. At one time there was no appeal at all from convictions under solemn procedure but this was remedied in 1926 and appeals are now heard by a bench of the Lord Commissioners of Justiciary.

The 'Not Proven' verdict continues to attract bemused attention from outside Scotland, and its existence is the result of a historical accident. However, if juries have the function (as they once had) solely of deciding whether certain facts had or had not been proved, their obvious verdicts were 'Proven' and 'Not Proven'. The illogicality arose when this was combined with a system under which a jury decided upon guilt or innocence on all the facts which emerged and were not confined to determining whether specific facts had been proved. While the present existence of three verdicts, 'Guilty', 'Not Guilty' and 'Not Proven', may be difficult to justify logically and while it would be highly unlikely that such a system would now be invented, in practice it works and provides a useful safety valve. 'Not Proven' verdicts are fairly rare and the alternative would often be conviction rather than acquittal.

Scottish criminal law has been well served by its writers. From Mackenzie's work in the 17th century, through Hume's classic *Commentaries* in the 18th and 19th centuries to Gordon's *Criminal Law* in the 20th century, Scotland has been blessed with writers of great analytical and practical skills whose works are held in high esteem. Even if the splendid Scots names for crimes, such as 'hamesucken' or 'stouthrief' are dropping out of use, the principles set out by our writers will guide Scots law for the foreseeable future.

MICHAEL C. MESTON

Michael Meston is currently Dean of the Faculty of Law of the University of Aberdeen. He has degrees in history from Aberdeen University and in law from Aberdeen and Chicago Universities. He has published books on the law of succession and on matrimonial homes. He is an honorary sheriff, a member of Grampian Health Board and has served as a trustee of the National Library of Scotland and of the National Museum of Antiquities of Scotland. He edited the editions of Lord Cooper's *Scottish Legal Tradition* until the preparation of this expanded work.

A Historical Perspective

INTRODUCTION

Two features particularly distinguish the history of Scots law when set beside that of other legal systems. The first is the great antiquity of the Scottish legal system, and the corresponding measure of continuity which can be traced from the earliest times of which there is any record right down to the present day. This is a characteristic which Scots law shares with English law, but in which it differs from the major systems of the Continent. In France and Germany, for example, the course of the law has been broken more than once by revolution. In addition, in each country the adoption of a written code—in France, the *Code Napoléon* of 1804, and in Germany, the BGB, or *Bürgerliches Gesetzbuch* of 1900—marked a break with the past of a different kind. In England and Scotland, by contrast, apart from the brief period of Commonwealth and Protectorate in the mid-17th century, there has been no revolution, nor has a written code of law been adopted to mark a new departure. In England there was a significant break in 1066, separating the Anglo-Saxon from the Anglo-Norman. In Scotland, however, there was no corresponding break between the Celtic past and Scoto-Norman feudalism. The history of Scots law, then, is one of great antiquity and continuity.

The second distinguishing feature is the ambivalent position which Scots law has long enjoyed between the two great legal traditions which have shaped the Western legal inheritance: on the one hand, the English (or Anglo-American) Common law, and on the other, the Civilian (or Romano-Germanic) legal tradition of the Continent. The Common law has evolved continuously since its early beginnings in the king's courts of 12th and 13th century England, and has steered a course independent to a surprising degree of outside legal influence. The Civilian tradition looks back to the Emperor Justinian's great codification of Roman law in 6th century Byzantium, the *Corpus Iuris Civilis*. To this tradition belong most, if not all modern European systems of law in the west, with the partial exception of Scandinavia. Scots law is unique in the extent to which it has drawn on and been influenced by both these great traditions throughout most of its long history.

This view of Scottish legal history, it must be admitted, differs sharply from that put forward by Lord Cooper in his celebrated original *Scottish Legal Tradition*, here reprinted. This is particularly true of the emphasis on continuity. Cooper wrote, indeed, that 'Scots Law is in a special sense the mirror of Scotland's history and traditions . . . and just as truly a part of our national inheritance as our language or literature or religion';[1] but he also wrote, 'There is a sense in which it is true to say that Scots Law has no history; for the continuity of its growth has been repeatedly interrupted and its story is a record of false starts and rejected experiments.'[2] The latter comment is quite misleading. Cooper sought to emphasise, in particular, the break in legal development caused by the Wars of Independence with England at the turn of the 13th and 14th centuries, and the fresh start signalled by the later 'Reception' of Roman law. In both cases, however, he exaggerated the element of change and underplayed the element of continuity.

The second main point of difference with Cooper is related to the first. Cooper, like the present writer, was concerned to emphasise the unique position of Scots law lying midway between the two great streams of European legal thought. He represented Scots law in the 12th and 13th centuries as being greatly influenced by the nascent English Common law, as indeed it was. But he suggested that the Wars of Independence caused a complete break with the past, and that the English Common law did not again influence the course of Scots law to any significant extent until after the Union of 1707. It is the writer's belief that Cooper underestimated the importance of the foundation laid in the 12th and 13th centuries as a basis for the future development of Scots law, and also the continuing, although admittedly reduced, role of the English Common law as a direct source of influence on Scots law between the Wars of Independence and the Union of 1707. Scots law has always been more of a hybrid than Cooper was prepared to admit, and the influence of the Civil or Roman law on Scots law has never operated in a context unaffected by the countervailing influence of the English Common law.[3]

CELTS AND SAXONS

The sources for the political history of Scotland before 1100 are sparse and difficult to interpret, and the sources for law and legal institutions doubly so. Nevertheless, it is clear that although a distinctively Scottish common law did not emerge until the 13th century, some of the component parts of that system can be traced back to a far more remote past.

In the Dark Ages there were four main political groupings in what is now Scotland; the Picts, the Scots of Dalriada, the Britons of Strathclyde and the Angles of the northern tip of the Anglo-Saxon kingdom of Northumbria. In the middle of the 9th century, the Picts, already long exposed to Scots Gaelic cultural influence, came under the kingship of Kenneth mac Alpin of the Dalriadic dynasty. Kenneth and his successors forged the kingdom of Alba, or Scotia, the forerunner of the later Scottish kingdom. This kingdom was at first restricted to Scotland north of the Forth, but expanded in the 10th and 11th centuries to incorporate both the British south west and the Anglo-Saxon south east.

Something can be deduced of the law of these four peoples. The Picts, although in many ways similar to their Celtic neighbours, appear to have operated a system of royal succession without parallel in Western Europe in historic times. Kings succeeded to the throne by virtue of their maternal rather than paternal kin. Thus, typically, a king would be succeeded by his brother (the son of his mother) or by his nephew (the son of his mother's daughter) rather than by his own eldest son or by a relative on his father's side. Anthropologists are familiar with such systems of matrilineal succession: they can still be found, for example, in the Indian state of Kerala and among the Ashanti of Ghana.[4] The law of the Britons appears to have resembled that of their P-Celtic-speaking cousins, the Welsh, whose native laws were later collected and attributed to Hywel Dda, a 10th-century South Welsh king.[5] The law of the Angles in Lothian and the Borders would have been a variant of Anglo-Saxon law, preserved in the Law Codes of kings from Ethelbert of Kent (d. 616) onwards, and in a number of contemporary legal documents.

The dominant influence in the early Scottish kingdom, however, was the Gaelic-speaking Scots. Here the relevant comparison is with Ireland, the original home of the Gaelic language and the Dalriadic dynasty.

31

Although little early legal material has survived in Scotland, the Irish record is rich. The Irish Law Tracts, some of them committed to writing as early as the 8th century, provide a fascinating picture of the operation of law in an archaic Celtic society. Much of the law concerns honour and status, and the avoidance of blood feuds arising from death or injury. There are sections on marriage and fosterage, on hostages, guarantors and sureties. The marriage law allowed for many different types of union of varying duration, and for ready divorce. Originally, indeed, it countenanced polygamy and concubinage. The custodians of early Irish law were a highly trained professional caste of jurists, the *breitheamhan* or 'brehons'—after whom these laws are sometimes referred to as the 'Brehon' laws. There is every indication that the law of the Gaelic-speaking Scots, first in Dalriada, and later in Alba, was similar to that of their compatriots in Ireland.[6]

One of the few Scots Gaelic texts to survive is the *Senchus Fer nAlban*, the 'Story of the Men of Scotland', compiled in the 7th century.[7] This lists the military strength of the various divisions of Dalriada and sets out the naval service due. Another early document which concerns Scotland as well as Ireland is *Cain Adomnain* (Adomnan's Law), a remarkable Dark Age Geneva Convention, negotiated about 697 AD by Adomnan, successor of Columba as abbot of Iona, and designed to protect women, children and non-combatants. The named guarantors of this 'law' include many contemporary Irish kings and clerics, and also Brude mac Derile, king of the Picts, two kings of Dalriada, and a bishop at Rosemarkie in the Black Isle.[8] Later, in the twelfth century, with the advent of the regular written record, bishops and monastic houses made written notes or *notitiae* of earlier land grants, some of which still survive. For example the Register of the Priory of St Andrews notes in Latin that Macbeth and his queen, Gruoch, had granted Kirkness by Loch Leven in Fife to the religious community, or Culdees, of St Serf.[9] One set of monastic *notitiae* provide particularly valuable evidence for our understanding of pre-feudal Scottish society, for they are written in Gaelic rather than in Latin. They record early land grants to the monastery of Deer in Buchan: thus, for example, 'Comgell son of Aed gave from Oirte as far as Puirene to Columba and to Drostan. Muiredach son of Morgann gave Pett MeicGartnait and the field of Toiche Teimne; and it is he who was mormaer and was toisech. Matain son of Cairell gave a mormaer's dues in Altrie and Cu Li son of Baithin gave a toisech's dues. . . .'.[10]

FOUNDATIONS

The 12th and 13th centuries saw the consolidation of the kingdom of Scotland, with the exception of the islands of Orkney and Shetland, and the forging of the Scottish national identity. They also saw the emergence of a distinctively Scottish common law.

The rise of the Scottish common law requires to be set in a wider European context. From the 11th century onwards there had been a revival of interest in legal studies throughout Europe. Towards 1100 Irnerius became the leading figure in the teaching of Roman law—that is, the law of Justinian's *Corpus Iuris*—at Bologna in northern Italy. The tradition of scholarship in Roman law has been continuous from his day until the present. At much the same time, again in Italy, the great edifice of the medieval Canon law, the *Corpus Iuris Canonici*, began to take shape. The Canon law owed much to the renewed study of Roman law; so much, indeed, as to justify the adage:

Legista sine canonibus parum valet
Canonista sine legibus nihil.

A Roman lawyer without Canon law is not worth much,
a Canon lawyer without Roman law nothing.

A third influence was feudal law. Unlike Roman law and Canon law, feudal law was never codified into an authoritative system, universally recognised throughout Western Christendom. Feudal rules were very adaptable and could accommodate many local variations. Nevertheless, the *Libri Feudorum*, the 'Books of the Feus' (*c.* 1150), of the Milanese jurist Obertus de Orto, proved widely influential, and were sometimes even regarded as a late and final addition to Justinian's *Corpus Iuris*.

Everywhere in Europe the new learned law interacted with older customary law. Scotland was no exception. In Scotland, however, as already noted, the customary base was partially Celtic, rather than purely Germanic. Although the Norman Conquest of 1066 did not extend to Scotland, the feudal law and institutions which found their way into Scotland were unmistakably Anglo-Norman. In Scotland, as in England—but unlike, for example, the situation in France and Germany—the rulers of the kingdom were able to shape a law which was largely national rather than local, co-terminous with the bounds of

33

their kingdom, a *common* law. In England, this common law was developed through precedents decided in the king's courts. In Scotland, the same was probably true, although surviving records are sparse. The Anglo-American Common law tradition can be traced back to the 'common law' developed by the kings of England in the 12th and 13th centuries. In Scotland the term 'common law', in the sense of the king's law, common to all his kingdom, is found already in the 13th century and has been in use ever since. Confusingly, the medieval European Civil and Canon lawyers also referred to their law as a 'common law'— *jus commune*—although here the reference was to the common learned law of Western Christendom.[11]

The Survival of Celtic Law. It is sometimes suggested that little, if anything, survived in Scotland of the older Celtic law into the feudal and post-feudal age. This is far from true. Traces of Celtic law survived for many centuries in the mainstream of later Scots law; and some customs, at one time regulated by Celtic law, continued to be observed in the Highlands until comparatively recent times. Thus the custom of fosterage lasted in the Highlands until the 18th century, and was commented on by Johnston and Boswell on their famous Hebridean tour. One long survival from the Celtic past was the payment of *cain*, a food render originally due to a lord in recognition of his authority. The obligation to render cain was written into many feudal charters and continued to be paid by vassals and tenants until quite modern times. Sometimes it merged with feu-duty. Cain was regularly paid in kind, and is sometimes referred to in later documents as 'cain fowl' or 'reek hen'—a hen from every lum that reeked. As late as last century, Lady Colquhoun of Luss kept a gauge to ensure that tenants presenting their cain of eggs did not tender any which were undersize![12]

One survival which mirrors the survival of Celtic law itself, gradually integrated until at length virtually unrecognisable, is that of the *breitheamh*, the professional judge or jurist of Celtic society. The *breitheamh* (Latin *iudex*) long survived the introduction of Scoto-Norman feudalism. He appears in the witness lists of early charters and is referred to in royal ordinances. He became, it would appear, a speaker of the customary law. Later he became the 'doomster' of court, the man who pronounced sentence or 'doom'. In the High Court of Justiciary, before the office of doomster was abolished in 1773, he doubled also as

34

executioner, a situation the dramatic potential of which was fully exploited by Sir Walter Scott in *The Heart of Midlothian*:

After Effie Deans has been found guilty of child-murder the doomster appears to pronounce sentence. 'When the doomster showed himself, a tall haggard figure arrayed in a fantastic garment of black and grey, passmented with silver lace, all fell back with a kind of instinctive horror.' The doomster then gabbles the sentence of death, and finishes thus: ' "And this", said the Doomster, aggravating his harsh voice, "I pronounce for doom." He vanished when he had spoken the last emphatic word, like a foul fiend after the purpose of his visitation has been accomplished.'

Even after the abolition of the office of doomster, the presiding judge at a murder trial in Scotland would conclude the sentence of death with the words 'which is pronounced for doom', thus linking himself, however tenuously, with the remote Celtic past.[13]

The Lordship of the Isles. In one part of Scotland, Celtic law continued to flourish in the later Middle Ages. After sovereignty over the Hebrides had been ceded by Norway to Scotland in 1266, the MacDonald descendants of Somerled (*d.* 1164) gradually consolidated their authority over the islands, from Islay in the south to Lewis in the north, and over much of the adjacent mainland as well. Their title in Gaelic was *Ri Innse Gall*, in Latin *Dominus Insularum* or 'Lord of the Isles'. The Lords of the Isles were patrons of the arts and of learning, and there is some evidence for a virtually independent legal structure, with judges or *breitheamhan* in the Gaelic tradition stationed on the larger islands, responsible to the administrative centre of the Lordship in Islay. The MacDonalds overreached themselves, however, and in the 15th and 16th centuries their principality was destroyed and annexed to the crown.[14]

The Common Law of Scotland. There was, therefore, no outright rejection of Celtic law, and the common law of Scotland has, in part at least, a Celtic base. However, the overwhelming influence on the development of the common law of Scotland in the 12th and 13th centuries was the Anglo-Norman law. This law was adopted or received by the kings of Scots themselves rather than imposed from without by conquest. Its influence was all pervasive in substantive law and procedure alike, and in the administration of justice. Its traces can be clearly seen in Scots law down to the present century.[15]

The main royal officer for the administration of justice at local level in Anglo-Norman England was the sheriff. The word itself—'shire-reeve'—is Anglo-Saxon, but the office was transformed under the Norman kings. The sheriff was first introduced into Scotland in the 12th century. By the end of the 13th, all of Scotland had been divided into sheriffdoms. It is ironic that in England, the country of origin, the sheriff's function gradually declined and is now mainly ceremonial, whereas in Scotland, the sheriff and his court continue to be a mainspring of judicial administration.

Another import from Anglo-Norman England was the office of justiciar. The justiciar was the king's *alter ego* in matters of justice, with extensive judicial powers, especially on the criminal side. In England, the office disappeared in the 13th century. Not so in Scotland. At first there were several justiciars in Scotland: one for Lothian; one for Galloway; and one for *Scotia* north of Forth. The office of justiciar north of Forth may have been assimilated with an earlier Celtic office of king's *breitheamh*. Eventually there was but one justiciar for the kingdom of the Scots, and he came to be styled the 'Lord Justice General'. The Lord Justice General remains Scotland's senior judge, presiding today over the High Court of Justiciary.[16]

A characteristic feature of the Anglo-Norman law was procedure by writ and inquest. The king would issue a judicial writ (Latin *breve*) directing the sheriff or some other officer of the law to hold an inquest, or jury, of prominent local men to determine the truth of some matter. Procedure by writ and inquest was also adopted in Scotland, and became equally characteristic of the early Scottish common law. For example, in 1261 king Alexander III directed a 'brieve' (as the writ was termed in later Scottish practice) to the sheriff of Forfar to make diligent and faithful inquiry by means of good and faithful men of the neighbourhood whether Margaret, Agnes, Suannoch, Christiana and Mariota, daughters of the late Simon, gatekeeper of Montrose castle, were his nearest and lawful heirs and entitled to succeed him in his office of gatekeeper and his lands of Inyaney.[17]

A record of 1428 shows the inquest being used to clarify an ancient usage with its roots in Celtic law. John of Spens, bailie of the crown lands of Glendochart in Perthshire, sitting with an inquest of fifteen, found that Finlay Dewar was the keeper of the *coigreach* of St Fillan—

that is, of the relic containing the saint's supposed pastoral staff—and that any inhabitant of Glendochart, whose goods or cattle had been stolen, could require Finlay to follow the goods throughout Scotland wherever they might be found, on payment of four pence, or a pair of shoes, and food for one night.[18]

Procedure by writ and inquest remained an integral part of English law until the 19th century. In Scotland, the procedure did not last so long in regular use, being gradually replaced from the 15th century onwards, save in a limited number of prescribed situations.[19] The prosecution of serious crime by way of 'indictment' before a jury was as distinctive a feature of Anglo-Norman criminal procedure as were the writ and inquest on the civil side. Here too Scots law borrowed in the 13th century from Anglo-Norman law, and retains to this day indictment and trial by jury in solemn criminal matters.

As was to be expected of a system rooted in feudalism, the influence of the Anglo-Norman law was greatest in matters concerning land or 'heritage'. From the time of king David I (1124–53), the feudal doctrine that the king was the ultimate lord (*dominus*) of all the land came gradually to prevail. All other landowners were 'vassals', holding their land at one remove or another from the king. The most honourable form of tenure was military tenure, known in later Scots law as 'ward holding', in which the return or *reddendo* for the land was strictly military, the service of so many knights—or, in the Gaelic west, naval, the service of a galley of so many oars. Thus William I (1165–1214) confirmed Seton, Winton and Winchburgh to Philip de Seton for the service of one knight, and David II (1329–71) granted Assynt in Sutherland to Torquil MacLeod for the service of a galley of 20 oars. Another honourable form of tenure, in which the required service was almost nominal, was known as 'blench ferme'. Thus the Campbells held Kilmun in Cowal for a pair of gloves to be tendered annually at the Glasgow Fair. A typical blench ferme render was one penny, 'if asked only' (*si petatur tantum*).

A distinctively Scottish form of tenure was 'feu ferme'. Here the *reddendo* was a money payment, or 'feu duty', generally payable twice a year at Whitsunday (15th May) and Martinmas (11th November). Despite the many reforming acts of recent years, feu ferme tenure remains the basis of landownership in Scots law today, and the legal relationship between 'vassal' and 'superior' still subsists, even if in many cases the actual feu duty has now been redeemed. Although the feudal

37

land law was originally adopted from Anglo-Norman England, Scots and English land law were never quite identical, and moved rapidly further apart after the legislation of Edward I (1272–1307) set English law on a fresh course. In England, for example, subinfeudation—the creation of a new feudal tenure by adding a further link to the feudal chain—was prohibited by Edward I in 1290. In Scotland, subinfeudation still remains competent more than 700 years later.

The law of succession to land was similar in both countries. Males were favoured to females in every degree of succession, and among males of equal degree the eldest succeeded. When succession did open to females, they shared equally. Typically, therefore, the eldest son took all. These rules were well established by the 14th century. They remained true of succession to land on intestacy in Scots law until 1964. The law of courtesy, which likewise survived until 1964, and had also been adopted originally from Anglo-Norman law, was an even more remarkable survival. Courtesy was the right which a widower enjoyed to a liferent of his deceased wife's estate. It could only be enjoyed, however, if a child had been born of the marriage, quick and living, and that child had been heard to cry. The reason for these peculiar rules was already a matter for debate in England in the 13th century; yet they remained part of Scots law until 1964! In 1368 Sir Thomas Erskine and Sir James Douglas of Dalkeith even fought a judicial duel before the king to determine whether a child had been stillborn, or born live and heard to cry; and whether, therefore, courtesy was exigible.[20]

By Medieval European standards the English monarchy was unusually strong and became centralised remarkably early. In England, the birth of the Common law was followed shortly by the establishment in the 13th century of central courts of justice, distinct from Parliament, and the emergence of a lay legal profession. In Scotland, however, a specialised central court and a lay legal profession did not begin to emerge until two hundred years later.

At local level the king's ordinary court was held by the sheriff, with more serious criminal business being reserved to the justiciar on his circuits (or 'justice-ayres') around the country. In royal burghs the burgh courts dispensed justice on the king's behalf. However, there were also many franchise courts in Scotland—courts of barony and courts of regality—in which local landowners exercised judicial rights on a hereditary basis. In highly centralised England such franchise courts, with a few exceptions, had ceased to exist by the end of the

13th century. In Scotland, by contrast, the heritable jurisdictions remained until 1748. The very greatest landowners, secular and religious, held their lands in regality. This jurisdiction, as the name implies, was semi-royal, and might include all the pleas of the crown, save only treason. Barony jurisdiction was more common, and included the much prized right of 'pit and gallows' (*furca et fossa*), which allowed the baron to sentence to death on his gallows tree or in his drowning pool those convicted of red-handed theft or slaughter. More typically, however, the baron court addressed itself to petty crime and to questions of good neighbourhood.[21]

The most important legal treatise to survive from the formative years of the Scottish common law is known from its opening words as *Regiam Majestatem*. Its date, its purpose and its authority as a source of Scots law have long been controversial. Much of the material in the *Regiam* is copied, with few alterations, from the English writer 'Glanvill', whose *De Legibus et Consuetudinibus Angliae* (The Laws and Customs of England) was composed at the end of the 12th century; but the *Regiam* also incorporates some later Romano-Canonical material. Lord Cooper originally dated the *Regiam* to *c.* 1230, and thought that it reflected the development of Scots law at that date. More recent research points to a date after—but perhaps not long after—1318, and urges caution as to how much can be deduced about the state of Scots law at any given moment from the text of *Regiam Majestatem*. If the latter date is correct, it certainly does not suggest that there was any conscious rejection of Anglo-Norman legal influence during or after the Wars of Independence. The *Regiam* may not have been fully official, but it does not seem to have been entirely private either. Although it has sometimes been rejected by our greatest legal writers as being no part of our law, there can be little doubt that *Regiam Majestatem* has, in practice, been regarded as a valid source of Scots law for over 500 years. Even in the 20th century it is occasionally cited in court.[22]

The Canon Law. The development of the common law and of the King's courts, however, is only part of the story. In medieval Scotland, as elsewhere in Western Christendom, jurisdiction was divided between secular authority and the Church. The Church looked to Rome and to the Canon law. During the 12th and 13th centuries the political power of the Papacy was at its height, and the law of the Church was developed by a succession of great lawyer Popes. It was codified in the

Corpus Iuris Canonici, the major elements in which are the *Decretum* of Gratian (*c.* 1150), and the *Decretals* of Pope Gregory IX (1234). From the 12th century onwards, the courts of the Church, staffed by expert clerical lawyers, and administering Canon law, existed alongside the king's courts. At diocesan level the ordinary court was the court of the Official, the ecclesiastical judge appointed by the bishop; but there might also be special 'judges-delegate' appointed *ad hoc* by Rome to resolve a particular dispute.[23]

The ambit of the Canon law was remarkably wide. It included questions of marriage and legitimacy; wills, testaments and executors; and obligations fortified by oath. Some commentators have suggested that the impact of the Canon law was so marked in 13th century Scotland that it completely overshadowed royal justice. Others have suggested conversely that the general Canon law was only accepted in Scotland according to equity and expediency; that Scotland, in some sense, had a Canon law of her own. Both opinions seem misconceived. Royal justice in Scotland, though not so highly centralised as in England, was far from inadequate for the country's needs.[24] As to the proposition that Scotland had a Canon law of her own, Maitland's answer to Stubbs, who asserted the same of Canon law in medieval England, seems apposite for Scotland also: 'It would have been as impossible for the courts Christian of this country to maintain . . . a schismatical law of their own as it would now be for a judge of the High Court to persistently disregard the decisions of the House of Lords: there would have been an appeal from every sentence, and reversal would have been a matter of course.'[25]

The 13th century did, however, mark the apogee of the power of the church. In that century judges-delegate might even determine questions touching on the ownership of land, later the most cherished preserve of the king's ordinary courts. The record of a series of litigations conducted before judges-delegate in the 1230s survives, concerning land attached to the church of Old Kilpatrick, near Dumbarton. It provides valuable evidence for the church courts in action as well as some memorable snapshots of contemporary life. The witness Alexander son of Hugh, for example, remembered seeing a man named Bede Ferdan, sixty years before or more, living on some of the disputed land, in a large house made of wattle beside the church of Kilpatrick to the east. Asked in whose name Bede possessed the land, he replied that it was in the name of the church; and that the only service required of Bede for the land was that he receive and feed all visitors to the church. A later witness, Gilbethoc, added the ominous information that Bede had been killed in defending the right and liberty of the church.[26]

The influence of the Canon law on later Scots law was longlasting and profound. Although the authority of the Pope was rejected at the Reformation, the authority of the Canon law continued save where expressly superseded. Thomas Craig, who practised law in the fifty years following the Reformation, noted in his *Jus Feudale* that 'in Scotland, notwithstanding that we have thrown off the papal yoke, the authority of the Canon Law endures: so much so, that where it differs from the Civil Law . . . we follow the Canon Law.'[27]

The influence of the Canon law was most obvious in the later Scots law of marriage and legitimacy. Canon law had recognised as valid, while condemning as irregular, marriages contracted *per verba de presenti*, that is, by a simple exchange of consents in the present tense, without the requirement of any further formality or the presence of a priest; and *per verba de futuro subsequente copula*, that is, by intercourse following on a promise to marry. Such marriages—sometimes, though incorrectly, referred to as 'handfast' marriages—survived in later Scots law until the Marriage (Scotland) Act of 1939. Ironically, the Roman Catholic Church had ceased to recognise them as valid in 1563, less than five years after the Scottish Reformation. The Canon law doctrine that a child, born illegitimate, might be legitimated by the subsequent marriage of its parents, so long as there had been no impediment at conception, was early accepted into the Scots common law. Indeed Robert III (1390–1406), born some years before his parents contracted a marriage valid in the eyes of the church, could hardly have succeeded otherwise. English law, by contrast, did not recognise legitimation by subsequent marriage until this century.

In other areas, too, Canon law influence was pervasive. Thus, although the Incest Act of 1567 referred to the 'word of God' and to Leviticus chapter 18, in practice the forbidden degrees of relationship continued to be interpreted according to the intricate rules of the medieval Canon law, save where expressly altered by statute. The consequences were dire. Whereas incest had formerly been merely an ecclesiastical offence, it became a crime after the Reformation, and a number of unfortunates were judicially executed by hanging, drowning or beheading on the most technical of grounds. In 1629, for example, John Weir was found guilty of 'the filthie and detestable cryme of incest', and sentenced 'to be tane to the Mercat Croce of Edinburgh and thair his heid to be strukin from his bodie.' His crime? He had married the widow of his great-uncle. In 1646 Jean Knox was hanged on the Castle Hill of Edinburgh because she had married John Murray when already five months pregnant to his brother William, 'committing thairby nottour and manifest incest express aganis the law of Almychtie God and Actis of Parliament'.[28]

The law of contract, too, was affected by the Canonists' insistence that an obligation seriously undertaken in good faith should be binding, even although there might be no reciprocal cause, consideration or *quid pro quo*. The greatest of our legal writers, Lord Stair, noted in his *Institutions* (1681) that a bare promise was binding in Scots law: 'Promises now are commonly held obligatory, the canon law having taken off the exception of the civil law, *de nudo pacto*.'[29] He also noted that Scots law demanded no particular form to constitute a binding contract because 'following rather the canon law . . . every paction produceth action'.[30] As a consequence the modern Scots law of contract, unlike English law, has no doctrine of consideration, and unlike some Civilian based systems, no notion of *causa*. The 18th century judge, Lord Hailes, was right to note that 'the canon law is not the law of Scotland; but the law of Scotland contains much of the canon law. This is so certain, that in many cases we determine according to the canon law without knowing it.'[31]

The debts owed by later Scots law to the Canon law were not confined to substantive law. Scots law also owes much to the personnel and the procedure of the Canon law. One consequence of the relatively late development of a legal profession and a central court was that churchmen trained in the Canon law continued to play an important part in the administration of lay as well as ecclesiastical justice. An outstanding example is William Elphinstone (1431–1514), Bishop of Aberdeen, and Keeper of the Great Seal. His first judicial appointment was as Official of Glasgow, but his later contribution to secular justice as a lord of the king's council, and as an Auditor of Causes and Complaints (a judicial committee of Parliament) over the long space of thirty five years was of crucial importance. In addition, Elphinstone, like many churchmen, had substantial judicial powers as a lord of regality in respect of the temporal possessions of his diocese.[32]

The evolution of the 'Romano-Canonical' procedure of the developed Canon law in the 12th and early 13th centuries has been described as 'one of the wonders of legal history'.[33] It was rational, it was written, and it advanced by orderly logical steps from proposition to proposition. Its influence on the history of Continental civil procedure can hardly be overestimated. In Scotland, too, thanks to Elphinstone and his ilk, its effects are clearly discernible in secular tribunals such as the council and the judicial committees of Parliament from at least the 15th century. When a supreme central court—the Court of Session— was finally established in the 16th century, its procedure was based on the Romano-Canonical model. To this day the procedure and terminology of the Court of Session clearly proclaim their Canon law origins.[34] From the Court of Session the new procedure spread to the sheriff court, and gradually the sheriff became more a judge in the canon law mould and less the chairman of a group of feudal landowners.

Udal Law. In 1468 and 1469 Scotland received first Orkney and then Shetland as pledges for the dowry of Margaret, princess of Norway and Denmark, and queen of James III. The pledge was never redeemed, and the United Kingdom now exercises full sovereignty over the Northern Isles. However, some traces of the islands' former law, based on the Gulathing Code of the Norwegian king Magnus 'the Law Mender' (1263–80) still survive.[35] This is particularly true of landownership, which in Norwegian law was allodial or 'udal', rather than feudal: that is, the landowner owned his land absolutely, and did not hold it, as in the feudal system, directly or indirectly of the Crown. Twice this century special rights attaining to udal ownership have been upheld—in respect of salmon fishing and the foreshore—and distinguished from the position under Scots law proper. A third attempt, which sought to establish special udal rights over buried treasure, failed but raised some fundamental questions concerning the nature of Crown sovereignty in the Northern Isles—questions which are currently being further explored in relation to salmon farming and the sea bed.[36]

RENAISSANCE AND REFORMATION

The Foundation of the Court of Session. Scots lawyers have always regarded 1532, the traditional date for the foundation of the Court of Session, as a key date in legal history. In that year Parliament passed the College of Justice Act 'Concerning the ordour of Justice and the institutioun of ane college of cunning and wise men for the administracioun of Justice'. This central civil court was to have a complement of fifteen judges, 'Lords of Council and Session' alias 'Senators of the College of Justice': seven lay lawyers and seven ecclesiastical under the presidency of a churchman. Some recent historians have doubted the significance of the events of 1532. They point to over one hundred years of earlier institutional development. In 1426 Parliament legislated for the holding of regular judicial sittings or 'sessions' to 'examine and finally determine all and sundry complaints causes and querellis that may be determined before the King's Council'. These 'sessions' appear to have been more spasmodic than regular, but throughout the 15th century there were further attempts to improve the quality of central justice through the king's council and the judicial committees of Parliament. By the end of the century in the reign of James IV, a specialist judicial body had begun to emerge within the council, the forerunner of the Lords of Council and Session. Fourteen of the fifteen judges appointed in 1532 had already sat on council sessions in 1531.

However, if the focus shifts from institutional development to jurisdictional competence, the importance of the establishment of the Court of Session as a College of Justice in 1532 becomes clearer. The Act gave the court authority 'to sitt and decyde apoun all actions civile', and the new body is soon found determining the most fundamental questions of feudal land law, that is, matters of 'fee and heritage'. This marked a radical new departure, as jurisdiction over fee and heritage had previously been a jealously guarded privilege of the ordinary feudal courts. Time and again in the 15th century the council and the Lords Auditors of Causes and Complaints had declined jurisdiction because it concerned fee and heritage. In 1471, for example, Robert Hamilton, provost of the collegiate church of Bothwell, raised an action before the Auditors touching the payment of mill dues, or 'multures', but was fined forty shillings, 'for his persute of the said matter quhare it aucht not to be folowit', because it concerned fee and heritage.[37]

Lord Cooper described the central judicial bodies of the late 15th century as 'Scotland's ersatz substitute for a supreme court'.[38] A better comparison can be made with the Chancellor's jurisdiction in England, which supplemented the common law and ordinary justice by providing extra-ordinary judicial remedies. In England, where the central courts of common law and a lay legal profession had been established since the 13th century, the supplementary jurisdiction of the Chancellor eventually gave rise to a system of 'Equity', distinct from common law. For hundreds of years, in England, 'Equity' in this technical sense ran parallel to common law, with its own courts, rules and judicial procedures. It was only with the Judicature Acts of 1873 and 1875 that the courts of equity and of common law in England finally merged. Even today, English lawyers think in terms of 'common law' rules and 'equitable' rules. In Scotland, however, in the much quoted words of the first Lord President Clyde, 'In the law of Scotland, law is equity and equity law, and when a Scots lawyer uses the term "common law", he uses it to distinguish it from Acts of Parliament.'[39] That this is so owes much to the establishment of 1532. The new court was much more than the old session writ large, for it combined the extra-ordinary equitable jurisdiction of the council with the ordinary common law jurisdiction over fee and heritage.[40]

The emergence of a central civil court in Scotland at this period can be viewed as part of a more general European pattern. In Germany, for instance, the *Reichskammergericht* was established in 1495 for the Holy Roman Empire. The slow evolution of a lay legal profession in Scotland in the 15th and 16th centuries also finds more ready parallels on the Continent than in England. It is possible to point to some laymen in the practice of law in Scotland in the mid-15th century and considerably more by 1500. However, lay lawyers remained overshadowed by churchmen until well into the 16th century. The first four Presidents of the Court of Session were all churchmen trained in Canon and Civil law.

The Reformation. The Scottish Reformation of 1559/60 brought to an end the old division between lay and ecclesiastical jurisdiction. In place of the courts of the Official new 'Commissary' courts were set up. Like their predecessors, these Commissary courts dealt with marriage and legitimation, wills, executors and moveable succession. They also had jurisdiction over divorce, now permitted on the grounds of desertion and adultery. Unlike their predecessors, however, and in contrast with the situation in England after the Reformation, these were lay courts, from which appeal ran after 1609 to the Court of Session. The courts of the Reformed Church—Kirk Session, Presbytery, Synod and General Assembly—were restricted increasingly, although not exclusively, to internal ecclesiastical matters.

45

Roman Law. The scope of the common law, then, increased greatly in the course of the 16th century. The establishment of the College of Justice in 1532 nipped in the bud any incipient division between common law and equity, and the extensive legal jurisdiction enjoyed by the church before the Reformation was largely transferred to secular courts. The development of the common law was also strongly affected by Roman law. Much Roman law—more than is generally realised— had already percolated by way of the Canon law. The humanist scholarship of the Renaissance saw a quickening of interest throughout Europe in the original texts of Justinian's *Corpus Iuris Civilis*. As a consequence, in many jurisdictions, Roman law came to exercise a more direct influence over the development of the law. Roman categories and Roman solutions supplemented and even supplanted the customary law. This stage in European legal history is often referred to as the 'Reception' of Roman law. English law remained comparatively unaffected by the Reception. Scots law corresponded more to the European norm. The late 16th century represents the high water mark of Roman influence. John Leslie, Lord of Session and Bishop of Ross, wrote in 1578, 'this far to the lawis of the Realme we are astricted, gif ony cummirsum or trubilsum cause fal out, as oft chances, quhilke can nocht be agriet be our cuntrey lawis, incontinent quhatevir is thocht necessar to pacify this controversie, is citet out of the Romane lawis'.[41]

This was undoubtedly an exaggeration. Scots land law remained firmly rooted in Anglo-Norman feudalism, and family law and procedure continued to develop on lines laid down by the Canon law. However, the terminology of Roman law came increasingly to pervade Scots law. For example, the legal rights of children, arising on the death of their parents, earlier known as 'bairns' part', were renamed 'legitim' after the *legitima portio* of Roman law. Some areas of law, such as moveable property and servitudes over land (*anglicé* 'easements') took on a decidedly Roman appearance, and writers on Scots law came increasingly to compare their native law with the Roman model.

Legislation. From the 15th century onwards many statutes were passed to enact new law, and not merely to reinforce and explain the old. The 19th century lawyer and historian, Cosmo Innes, wrote of 'those brief, terse statutes which shame the legislation of a later wordy age'.[42] A surprising number of these acts remained on the statute book until the late 20th century. Lord Cooper wrote in 1951 of 'a long succession of

46

pivotal reforms around which whole chapters of Scots law continued to revolve for centuries and many of which are still in force'.[43] Since Cooper wrote many of these ancient statutes have been repealed. The Prescription Acts of 1469, 1474 and 1579 disappeared with the Prescription and Limitation (Scotland) Act of 1973. The Marriage and Incest Acts of 1567 were repealed in 1977 and 1986 respectively, four hundred years too late. The Bankruptcy Acts of 1621 and 1696 were repealed, but largely re-enacted, by the Bankruptcy (Scotland) Act of 1985. The earliest act to remain on the statute book is the Royal Mines Act of 1424, which reserves gold and silver found in the ground to the crown. Important acts still in force are the Leases Act of 1449/50, which remains the foundation of the law of leases in Scotland, the Subscription of Deeds Acts of 1579 and 1681, and the Registration Act of 1617 which set up the Register of Sasines to record deeds conveying title to land.[44]

Legal Writing. The late 16th and early 17th centuries saw the rise of Scottish legal writing. The *Jus Feudale* of Thomas Craig (1538–1608), which expounds the feudal land law of Scotland and compares it with English law, setting both in a broad European context, is the first of a series of works still regarded as authoritative by the Scottish courts today. Craig was a jurist of European stature, a pioneer of the historical and comparative method, whose reputation has recently been rehabilitated by modern historical scholarship.[45] Another Scottish jurist with a European reputation was William Wellwood (*d.* 1622), whose *Sea Law of Scotland* 'shortly gathered and plainly dressit for the reddy use of all sea-faring men' appeared in 1590, and his *Abridgement of All Sea Laws* in 1613. Of more purely Scottish interest are the works of Sir John Skene, Lord Clerk Register (*d.* 1617). He was concerned that the wording and terminology of the older Scottish law was becoming obscure and unintelligible to his contemporaries, and was in danger of being displaced by Roman law. Skene's legal glossary, *De Verborum Significatione*, published in 1597, has recently been described as 'a magnificent legal dictionary . . . a goldmine whose riches extend far beyond the strictly legal'.[46] Skene's greatest achievement was his edition of the key medieval text *Regiam Majestatem*, together with others of the 'auld lawes', published in both Latin and Scots in 1609.

CONSOLIDATION

Throughout Europe from the 16th century onwards, as the modern nation state emerged, systematic and analytical treatises consolidating the work of the Reception and expounding the law on a national basis began to appear. Such works were sometimes entitled 'Institutes' or 'Institutions' after the famous *Institutes* of the Emperor Justinian. An early example is Guy Coquille's *Institution au Droit Français* published in 1607. Later examples are Selchow's *Institutiones Iurisprudentiae Germanicae* (1757), and Asso and Manuel's *Instituciones del Derecho Civil de Castilla* (1771). Scotland fits well into this European pattern, although in modern Scottish legal parlance the term 'Institutional' has come to be applied to a small canon of works on Scots law, starting with Craig's *Jus Feudale*, which are regarded as having particular authority. A leading Continental legal historian has recently suggested that it would be appropriate to use the term in its original and primary meaning, and refer to the 'Institutional phase' of European legal history.[47]

During the 16th and 17th centuries the academic writings of Craig and Skene were complemented by more practical manuals on the law, often known simply as 'Practicks'. John Sinclair (*d.* 1566), Bishop of Brechin and Lord President of the Court of Session, compiled an early set of Practicks. The best known Practicks are those of Sir James Balfour of Pittendreich (*d.* 1583), who was, like Sinclair, Lord President of the Court of Session, and of Sir Thomas Hope (*d.* 1646), Lord Advocate to Charles I.[48] Balfour's *Practicks*, though hardly systematic, are an invaluable guide to the practice of law in the later 16th century. References to the 'auld lawes' and to *Regiam Majestatem* rub shoulders with decisions of the Court of Session in titles such as 'Marriage', 'Tocher', 'Beggars', 'Bastards' and 'Muirburn'.

Stair. At the end of the 17th century theory and practice were triumphantly combined in the most influential work ever written on Scots law, *The Institutions of the Law of Scotland*, by James Dalrymple, Viscount of Stair (1619–95), published in 1681. Stair, like Sinclair and Balfour, was able to draw on his experience as Lord President of the Court of Session. His *Institutions* fit comfortably into the European mould—the systematic exposition of a national legal system—and are universally accepted as the greatest of Scotland's 'Institutional' writings.

Lord Cooper's celebrated encomium bears repetition: 'The publication of his *Institutions* in 1681 marked the creation of Scots law as we have since known it—an original amalgam of Roman Law, Feudal Law and native customary law, systematised by resort to the law of nature and the Bible, and illuminated by many flashes of ideal metaphysic. To this work and its author every Scots lawyer has since paid a tribute of almost superstitious reverence, and the resort still occasionally made to Stair in the House of Lords and the Privy Council suggests that it is not only in the estimation of his fellow-countrymen that he falls to be ranked amongst the great jurists of all time.'[49] Recent studies of Stair's work, including those by scholars outwith Scotland, have served only to emphasise the magnitude of Stair's achievement.[50]

Stair was the architect of modern Scots law, and in that sense his work marks a new beginning. Yet it was also very much a consolidation of what had gone before. Stair himself would have rejected any suggestion that he had cut loose from the past. Time and again he refers to Craig and cites decisions of the Court of Session to support a proposition. He himself collected and published the decisions of the Court of Session from 1661 to 1681. In the preface to his second edition of 1693 he writes, 'I have been very sparing to express my own opinion in dubious cases of law, not determined by our custom and statutes, but have rather congested what the Lords [of Session] have done . . . But I have used more freedom in opening the fountains of law and justice, and the deductions thence arising, by the law of nature and reason.'

The last sentence is significant. Stair believed that the essence of law derived ultimately from equity and morality, rather than from power and authority: 'Equity is the body of the law, and the statutes of men are but as the ornaments and vestiture thereof.'[51] In keeping with this view, be regarded Roman law, which he cited frequently in his *Institutions*, as a rule or system not binding for its authority, but to be followed rather for its equity. It is interesting to note that Thomas Craig before him, in his *Jus Feudale*, had adopted the same attitude towards Roman law as a source: 'In our own realm of Scotland we use the Roman Law so far as it appears to us to be consonant with natural equity and reason.'[52]

Mackenzie. Contemporary with Stair was Sir George Mackenzie (1636–91), King's Advocate, a strong supporter of the royal prerogative, and more inclined than Stair to view law as a command. Mackenzie was a considerable scholar and prolific writer, the author of *Aretina*, which has some claim to be regarded as the first Scottish novel, as well as many works on literature and law. His *Institutions of the Law of Scotland* (1684) is essentially a short primer, which nevertheless provides an instructive counterpoint to Stair's great work. Mackenzie's *Law and Customs of Scotland in Matters Criminal* (1678), deeply imbued with Civilian learning, is a treatise on an altogether larger scale, and marks an important stage in the exposition of Scotland's criminal law.

The Criminal Procedure Act. One act of the last Scots Parliament, which sat from 1689 until the Union of 1707, deserves special mention: the Criminal Procedure Act of 1701, repealed and effectively re-enacted in 1887 and again in 1975. Scots law knows neither Magna Carta nor Habeas Corpus, but the 1701 Act laid down important safeguards against detention without trial. No-one can be detained in custody for more than 80 days unless an indictment has been served; or more than 110 days unless trial has commenced. Otherwise the charge is dropped and cannot be brought again. These salutary rules are striking enough in their original context, but still appear remarkable in late 20th century Europe, where far longer periods of detention without trial are a commonplace, even in England.

The Union of 1707. In 1603, on the death of Queen Elizabeth, James VI of Scotland succeeded to the English throne. The 'Union of the Crowns', however, had little direct effect on the development of Scots law. King James did, indeed, promote a scheme for the harmonisation of Scots and English law, but, in the event, little came of it or of similar proposals later in the 17th century.[53] Personal union was followed by political union in 1707. In that year the Parliament of Scotland passed the Act of Union with England, and the English Parliament passed the Act of Union with Scotland. As a consequence, the new United Kingdom of Great Britain came into being on 1st May 1707. The Acts of Union contained important safeguards for Scots law. No alteration was to be made in the laws concerning 'private Right'—'except for the evident utility of the subjects within Scotland'.[54] The Court of Session and the High Court of Justiciary (which had been established in 1672) were to remain within Scotland in all time coming; and no Scottish cases were to be 'cognoscible by the Courts of Chancery, Queens-Bench, Common-Pleas, or any other Court in Westminster-hall'.[55] This provision did not prevent appeals being taken from the Court of Session to the House of

Lords, nor was it intended to.[56] All laws and statutes contrary to, or inconsistent with the terms of the Articles of Union were to be void.[57] The status of these provisions and their relation to the doctrine of the sovereignty of parliament has often been debated. According to the English constitutional theorist, Dicey, writing last century, 'neither the Act of Union with Scotland nor the Dentists Act 1878, has more claim than the other to be considered as supreme law'.[58] However, Professor John Mitchell concluded that, as regards some at least of the provisions of the Act of Union, the element of entrenchment was apparent. He put the question, 'Was Parliament born unfree?'[59] Lord Cooper made a notable contribution to the discussion in the leading case of *MacCormick* v *Ld Advocate* in 1953, in which he said, 'The principle of the unlimited sovereignty of Parliament is a distinctively English principle which has no counterpart in Scottish Constitutional law.'[60] (See also the Appendix, page 98.) The debate continues.[61]

The '45. The aftermath of the 1745 Rebellion saw the passing of the Heritable Jurisdictions Act which brought to an end the courts of regality and stripped the baron courts of most of their power. It came into force on 25 March 1748, a date which has recently been described as one 'which should rank with the Union of the Crowns in 1603 and the Union of the Parliaments of 1707 in the slow destruction of the traditional Scottish polity'.[62] In this case, at least, the destruction was all to the good.

The Eighteenth Century. The 18th century has been described as the Classical Age of Scots law. There was little statute law reform, but the tradition of institutional writing continued. Andrew M'Dowall, Lord Bankton, published his *Institutes* in 1751 in which he expressly compared Scots with English law. *An Institute of the Law of Scotland*, the major work of John Erskine (1695–1768), professor of Scots law at the University of Edinburgh, appeared posthumously in 1773. Erskine's shorter *Principles of the Law of Scotland* (1st ed., 1754) succeeded Sir George Mackenzie's *Institutions* as a student primer, and was not itself displaced until the 20th century by Gloag and Henderson's *Introduction to the Law of Scotland*. Erskine is cited more frequently in the Court of Session today than Stair, perhaps because he is nearer in time, perhaps because his language is less opaque. At the beginning of the 19th century George Joseph Bell (1770–1843), like Erskine, professor of Scots law at the University of Edinburgh, contributed his *Commentaries on the Mercantile Jurisprudence of Scotland* (1804). If Erskine's *Institute* looked backwards as a consolidation or apotheosis of the feudal land law, Bell's *Commentaries*, constructed around the topic of bankruptcy, looked forward to Scotland's industrial and mercantile future. Stair, Erskine and Bell are generally held to be the greatest writers on Scots private law, although this judgement may underestimate Craig and Bankton. At the end of the 18th century, the *Commentaries on the Law of Scotland respecting Crimes* (1797) of David Hume (1756–1838), Baron (judge) of the Court of Exchequer, and, like Erskine and Bell, professor of Scots law at Edinburgh University, provided the classic statement of Scottish criminal law.

The 18th century marked the highpoint of the Faculty of Advocates. Advocates and judges dominated polite society, and made notable contributions to the 'Scottish Enlightenment'. The achievements of the Enlightenment belong more to the history of ideas than to the history of Scots law.[63] However, the legal writing of Henry Home, Lord Kames (1696–1782), particularly his *Historical Law Tracts* (1758) and *Principles of Equity* (1760), had a considerable impact on the domestic Scottish scene, besides being widely read in England, the Continent and America. Kames's *Principles of Equity*, indeed, is still cited occasionally as an authority in the Scottish courts. Some advocates, such as James Boswell and Sir Walter Scott, achieved great fame outwith the law. Others moved south to practise at the English bar, two of them, Alexander Wedderburn (1733–1805) and Henry Brougham (1778–1868) attaining the office of Lord Chancellor. One of the greatest of all English judges, William Murray, Lord Mansfield, Lord Chief Justice of the King's Bench from 1756 to 1788, was also a Scot, although his legal training took place entirely in England.

Codification. Towards the end of the 18th century there was a movement on the Continent for the codification of law. A civil code was issued for Bavaria in 1756, and a code for Prussia in 1794, In 1804 Napoleon promulgated his famous *Code Civil*. Scots law, too, was ready for codification: it had been expounded systematically and succinctly by a succession of gifted writers, and the long static years of the 18th century, relatively free of law reform, had aided consolidation. Yet Scots law has never been codified. The reason why must be ascribed, at least in part, to Union with England, and to the absence of a competent legislative assembly in Scotland itself. As a consequence, the continuity of Scots law has remained unbroken to an extent surprising to a Continental lawyer.

THE MODERN LAW

The law of the 18th century is now remote from the modern practitioner, and the medieval law an arcane mystery. From the early 19th century onwards, however, much remains which is familiar. Hume's *Commentaries* had consolidated the criminal law, and Bell's *Commentaries* the civil. By 1830, after some decades of reform, the Court of Session had assumed its present aspect, both as regards form— an Inner and an Outer House, the former being comprised of two Divisions—and as regards procedure. Nineteenth-century cases are cited regularly in the courts today. It is not, then, entirely surprising that Lord Cooper ended his historical survey about 1820. 'That may seem a long time ago', he wrote in 1949, 'but the purpose of history is not to chronicle events but to isolate and interpret controlling tendencies; and we are still too near the trees of the 19th century to see the wood. In law the last one hundred and twenty years belong to the dynamic present rather than to the historic past'.[64]

Nevertheless, Cooper did point to two leading characteristics of the modern period, both of which he disliked. There would probably be general agreement as to the first, the ever increasing volume of statute law and delegated legislation, or, as Cooper put it, 'the formidable and still rising torrent of acts, regulations and orders . . . the subject of many an unavailing protest from lawyers and laymen alike'.[65] Since the mid 19th century, not least in the last twenty five years, a steady stream of legislation has reformed many core areas of private law and transformed some almost out of recognition. Areas most affected include land law and the law of succession, and family law in all its aspects. So extensive indeed have been the changes that it would scarcely be possible to write now, as Cooper did, that 'as in 1820 the great bulk of the law of Scotland is still common law—improved, simplified and modified in details, but in essence the same'.[66] There has been much statutory reform, too, of commercial law.

Not all the changes in private law have been the consequence of legislative reform. The law of obligations—contract, delict (*anglicé* tort) and unjust enrichment—has developed largely through the slow operation of the common law, that is, by decisions reached by the courts in particular cases on the basis of past precedent and legal principle. Important areas of criminal law also, such as homicide and theft, have remained dominated by the principles of the common law. One example is the concept of diminished responsibility, developed and refined by the Scottish common law in the 19th and 20th centuries, and only introduced into English criminal law by statute in 1957.

Lord Cooper was particularly disparaging about the content of much modern law, referring to 'vast tracts of so-called "law"', and to 'sub-legal matters' containing no more than 'a faint tincture of juristic principle'.[67] He had in mind areas such as income tax, social security and local government. Here too the torrent has continued unabated since he wrote. Although the insidious growth of delegated legislation remains a cause for concern, in some respects Cooper's comments now appear rather high-minded. The distinction between public and private law no longer seems as clear as once it did; and new classifications of law which combine both public and private, such as 'consumer law' and 'labour law' have become widely accepted. It would be unrealistic to dismiss these as 'sub-legal'. One important development in public law has been the recent growth of the procedure of 'judicial review', by which the administrative actings of public bodies have been brought under close scrutiny by the courts.

The second leading characteristic which Lord Cooper discerned in the development of the modern law was the ever-rising influence of English law, not, as he put it, 'through the conscious pursuit by Scots lawyers of a desirable foreign contact', which would have been quite acceptable, even beneficial, 'but unsought and indirect'.[68] He complained of 'the haphazard inoculation of one system with ideas taken from another'.[69] There were two main channels of this English influence. The first was the process by which, in Cooper's view—and having been Lord Advocate he was in a position to know—Scottish legislation was all too often initiated. A statute might be drafted in London by English lawyers, thinking in English legal categories, and with the English legal system in mind. Only at the last minute, and with a minimum of alteration, would it be 'adapted' to Scottish use. Such haphazard legislation with its roots in another legal system could not be conducive to the smooth running and orderly development of Scots law. The comments of Lord Dunedin in *Governors of George Heriot's*

Trust v *Caledonian Railway Company* in 1915 on the Lands Clauses Consolidation (S) Act of 1845 provide one example out of many to illustrate Cooper's complaint: 'The genesis of the 1845 Act is plain enough. It is a copy of the English Act of the same year, the copy being adapted to Scottish needs by a person with a very hazy notion of Scottish real property law. Indications of ignorance crop up all through the statute, in small things as well as great.'[70]

The second channel for English influence was to be found in the decisions of the House of Lords. After the Union of 1707 the House of Lords became the supreme court of appeal from Scotland in civil matters. Yet it was not until 1876, with the passing of the Appellate Jurisdiction Act, that there was any provision for the presence there of judges trained in Scots law. Even then they were almost invariably outnumbered in any given appeal by their English-trained counterparts. The results could hardly be beneficial to Scots law as, inadvertently or otherwise, legal concepts appropriate to one system were applied to another through binding decisions at the highest level. A notorious example which illustrates this complaint of Cooper occurs in the speech of Lord Chancellor Cranworth in 1858 in *Bartonshill Coal Company* v *Reid*. This case decided that the 'doctrine of common employment', already accepted in English law, was also the law in Scotland. The doctrine prevented a workman, injured in the course of his employment through the negligence of a fellow employee, from suing his employer in delict, on the fiction that by taking employment in the first place he had accepted the risk that a fellow employee might be negligent. The doctrine remained part of both English and Scots law until its abolition by statute in 1947. In *Bartonshill*, Lord Cranworth reviewed the English case law and then continued, 'I consider . . . that in England the doctrine must be regarded as well settled; but if such be the law of England, on what ground can it be argued not to be the law of Scotland? The law, as established in England, is founded on principles of universal application, not on any peculiarities of English jurisprudence.'[71]

Undoubtedly Lord Cooper was right to point to English influence as a major factor in the development of Scots law since the early 19th century. Undoubtedly, too, he was right to warn of the perils of uncritical acceptance, and the dangers inherent in a legislative and judicial structure so dominated by a powerful neighbour. His criticism of the legislative procedure in particular has often found an echo since he wrote. In 1974, for example, Professor David Walker wrote of the

Consumer Credit Bill (later Act) of that year: 'The Bill is just another piece of the extinction of Scots law by draftsmen, officials, Ministers and a Parliament who neither know nor care about Scots law.'[72] Lord Cooper, a keen Unionist, did not go on to point the moral that it is difficult to serve a legal system adequately without a distinct legislature; but others have found in the quixotic current position a strong argument for devolution. Scots law stands almost alone in the world as a legal system without a legislature within the jurisdiction. The danger of being shunted down a branch line is all too clear.

In some respects, however, it can be argued that Cooper overdrew the picture of the baneful influence of English jurisprudence. Not all English influence came 'unsought and indirect'. Not all of it has been inimical to the regular development of Scots law. In some areas, such as defamation and trusts, English doctrines have been harmonised with Scots in the best eclectic tradition of the Scottish common law. Sometimes prior English legislation has provided a stalking horse for later Scots reform, as in the case of divorce for irretrievable breakdown. Sometimes, of course, the process has operated in reverse, notoriously so in the case of the community charge or 'poll tax'.

English lawyers, too, tend to be more sensitive now to the existence of a separate system north of the Border. The borrowing of the concept of diminished responsibility into English criminal law this century from Scots has already been noted. More recently, the Crown Prosecution Service has been established in England and Wales partly on the Scottish model. The House of Lords in its judicial capacity, anomalously constituted though it may be, attracts little criticism now from Scotland. This may be partly due to the long and distinguished contribution of Lord Reid to British justice as a Scots Lord of Appeal from 1947 to 1971. One might almost say that the boot is now on the other foot with the appointment for the first time of a practising Scots lawyer, Lord Mackay of Clashfern, in 1987, as Lord Chancellor of Great Britain.

The decades since Cooper wrote, and, especially the last twenty five years, have been marked by a great transformation in Scots law, greater perhaps than in any period of similar duration since the 12th and 13th centuries. Much of the law with which Cooper was familiar has now been wholly superseded. There have been far reaching reforms in both public and private law. On the constitutional front, too, the landscape is rapidly changing. The United Kingdom has been a member of the

Council of Europe since its inception in 1949, and of the European Economic Community since 1973. As a member of the former, Britain recognises the jurisdiction of the European Court of Human Rights at Strasbourg, and as a member of the latter that of the Court of Justice of the European Communities at Luxemburg. The first British judge appointed to the Court of the European Communities, subsequently President of the Court, was a Scots lawyer, Lord Mackenzie Stuart. The possibility of a Bill of Rights is regularly canvassed. The Scotland Act of 1979 promised a devolved assembly for Scotland, but was never implemented. However, devolution is once again on the political agenda.

Despite this transformation, to quote for the last time from Lord Cooper, 'the anchors of the common law of Scotland have not yet dragged'.[73] If anything, Scots law is in better heart, and Scots lawyers more conscious of their proud and independent legal tradition than when Cooper wrote. That this is so is in no small measure due to the inspired leadership of Lord Cooper himself, and of his principal disciple, the late Sir Thomas Smith. Landmarks in the rejuvenation of Scots law and legal scholarship include the founding in 1949 of the Law Society of Scotland, the establishment in 1960 of the Scottish Universities Law Institute with a remit to publish works on Scots law, and the setting up in 1965 of the Scottish Law Commission. A more recent initiative, *The Laws of Scotland: Stair Memorial Encyclopaedia*, the first volume of which appeared in 1987, promises to become the classic statement of the law of Scotland at the close of the 20th century. The law faculties of the Scottish Universities have also played their part. The honours degree in law was introduced in the 1960s, and writing on Scots law, much of it centred on the Universities, but also—and this is a sign of vitality— coming from practitioners, is as buoyant now as at any time in its history. The European connection has drawn attention to rather than detracted from the separate standing of Scots law. With its Civilian credentials secure and its Common law credentials acknowledged Scots law is well placed to play a part, albeit a modest one, in any movement towards European harmonisation. The last Lord Chancellor of an independent Scotland, Lord Seafield, is reported to have said when he heard of the passing of the Act of Union in 1707, 'Now there is ane end of ane auld sang'. So far at least as the law of Scotland is concerned, his words were happily premature.

ENDNOTES

1.   T. M. Cooper, *The Scottish Legal Tradition* (Saltire Society, Edinburgh 1949) 5. (see also *infra* p. 65)

2.   T. M. Cooper, *Select Scottish Cases of the 13th Century* (Edinburgh and London 1944) lxi.

3.   Apart from *The Scottish Legal Tradition* and *13th Century Cases*, above mentioned, Lord Cooper's views on the course of Scottish legal history can be conveniently studied in his David Murray Lecture at Glasgow University, 'The Dark Age of Scottish Legal History, 1350–1650' (1951), reprinted in the Rt. Hon. Lord Cooper of Culross, *Selected Papers* (Edinburgh 1957) 219–36; in his edition of *Regiam Majestatem* for the Stair Society (Edinburgh 1947); and in 'From David I to Bruce, 1124–1329: The Scoto-Norman Law', chapter one in the Stair Society's *Introduction to Scottish Legal History* ed. G. C. H. Paton (Edinburgh 1958). J. H. Baker, *An Introduction to English Legal History* (3rd ed., London 1990) can be thoroughly recommended on English law, and Robinson, Fergus and Gordon, *An Introduction to European Legal History* (London 1985) helps to place the history of Scots law in a European context.

4.   There is a large literature on the Picts and the hypothesis of matrilineal succession. Alfred P. Smyth launches an attack on the hypothesis in his *Warlords and Holy Men* (London 1984, reprinted Edinburgh 1989). W. D. H. Sellar, 'Warlords, Holy Men and Matrilineal Succession' (1985) 36 *Innes Review* 29–43 attempts to refute Smyth.

5.   For Welsh law see now Dafydd Jenkins, *The Law of Hywel Dda* (Gomer Press, Llandysul 1986).

6.   Fergus Kelly, *Guide to Early Irish Law* (Dublin 1988) provides a long awaited introduction to Irish law. For the law of the Gaelic speaking Scots see, *inter alia*, W. F. Skene, *Celtic Scotland* 3 vols. (2nd ed., Edinburgh 1886–90); John Cameron, *Celtic Law* (Edinburgh 1937); John Bannerman, 'The Scots of Dalriada' in *Who are the Scots* ed. Gordon Menzies (London 1971 and reprints) 66–79, and 'The Lordship of the Isles' in *Scottish Society in the Fifteenth Century* ed. J. Brown (London 1977) 209–40; G. W. S. Barrow, 'The Lost Gaidhealteachd of Medieval Scotland' in *Gaelic and Scotland* ed. W. Gillies (Edinburgh 1989) 67–88; and W. D. H. Sellar, 'Celtic Law and Scots Law: Survival and Integration' 29 *Scottish Studies* (1989) 1–27.

7.   John Bannerman, *Studies in the History of Dalriada* (Edinburgh and London 1974) 27–156.

8.   Mairin Ni Dhonnchadha, 'The Guarantor List of Cain Adomnain, 697' *Peritia* vol 1 (1982) 178–215.

9.   *Liber Cartarum Prioratus Sancti Andree in Scotia* (Bannatyne Club 1841) p. 114; *Early Scottish Charters prior to 1153* ed. A. C. Lawrie (Glasgow 1905) no. V.

10.   Kenneth Jackson, *The Gaelic Notes in the Book of Deer* (Cambridge 1972) 33–4 and passim.

11.   The varying ways in which the expression 'common law' is used, according to context, are thoroughly confusing. In this essay, the spelling 'Common law' is reserved for the English legal system and the Anglo-American Common law tradition. But the term 'common law' is also used within that tradition in a technical sense to distinguish 'common law' from 'equity', and to distinguish both from statute. In modern Scots law, as will appear (*infra* p. 74; *cf.* p. 45 *supra.*), no distinction is drawn between equity and (common) law, and the expression 'common law' is used in distinction to statute.

12.   Gordon Donaldson, *Sir William Fraser* (Edinburgh 1985) 26.

13.   *Sheriff Court Book of Fife 1523–1542* ed. W. C. Dickinson (Scottish History Society 1928) lxv–lxix; G. W. S. Barrow, 'The Judex' 1966 *Scottish Historical Review* 16–26, reprinted in Barrow *The Kingdom of the Scots* (London 1973) 69–82; and W. D. H. Sellar, 'Celtic Law and Scots Law' (*supra* note 6).

14.   For the Lordship of the Isles see *inter alia* John Bannerman, 'Lordship' (*supra* note 6) and 'The Lordship of the Isles: Historical Background' in *Later Medieval Monumental Sculpture in the West Highlands* edd. K. A. Steer and J. W. M. Bannerman, (London 1977) Appendix II; and *Acts of the Lords of the Isles 1336–1493* edd. R. W. and Jean Munro (Scottish History Society 1986).

15.   W. D. H. Sellar, 'The Common Law of Scotland and the Common Law of England' in *The British Isles 1100–1500: Comparisons Contrasts and Connections* ed. R. R. Davies (Edinburgh 1988) 82–99.

16.   G. W. S. Barrow, 'The Scottish Justiciar in the 12th and 13th Centuries' 1971 *Juridical Review* 97–148, reprinted in *The Kingdom of the Scots* 83–138, is now the standard account of the early history of the justiciar.

17.   *The Acts of the Parliaments of Scotland [APS]* edd. T. Thomson and C. Innes (Edinburgh 1814–75) 100; and Cooper, *13th Century Cases* no. 56.

18.   *Royal Commission on Historical Manuscripts* (London 1870–   ) 4th Report, 514a; and see, *inter alia*, W. A. Gillies, *In Famed Breadalbane* (Perth 1938 and reprint) 64–73. The *coigreach* still exists: it was gifted to the Society of Antiquaries of Scotland last century, and at the time of writing (1989) is on display in Edinburgh in the exhibition 'Scotland—The Wealth of a Nation'.

19. There has been much recent research on process by brieve in Scots law: see, for example, Hector L. MacQueen, 'Pleadable Brieves, Pleading and the Development of Scots Law' 4 *Law and History Review* (1986) 403–22. Hector McKechnie's David Murray Lecture *Judicial Process upon Brieves, 1219–1532* (Glasgow University 1956) is the essential starting point, and deals specifically with the later survivals.

20. W. D. H. Sellar, 'Courtesy, Battle and the Brieve of Right, 1368—a story continued' in *Miscellany II* of the Stair Society, ed. Sellar (1984) 1–12.

21. Dickinson's *Sheriff Court Book of Fife (supra* note 13), and his *Court Book of the Barony of Carnwath 1523–1542* (Scottish History Society 1937) remain the standard accounts of these courts. Dickinson's *Early Records of the Burgh of Aberdeen 1317, 1398–1407* (Scottish History Society 1957) is a valuable contribution on the burgh court. For regality courts see *Regality of Dunfermline Court Book 1531–1538* edd. J. M. Webster and A. A. M. Duncan (Dunfermline 1953).

22. A. A. M. Duncan, 'Regiam Majestatem: A Reconsideration' 1961 *Juridical Review* 199–217; Peter Stein, 'The Romano-canonical part of Regiam Maiestatem' 1969 *Scottish Historical Review* 107–23; Alan Harding, 'Regiam Majestatem amongst Medieval Law-Books' 1984 *Juridical Review* 97–111. The *Regiam* was cited in *Ld Advocate v University of Aberdeen and Budge* (The St Ninian's Isle Treasure Case) 1963 SC 533.

23. Cooper, *13th Century Cases*; and Simon Ollivant, *The Court of the Official in Pre-Reformation Scotland* (Stair Society 1982).

24. Barrow's 'Scottish Justiciar' (*supra* note 16), especially pages 85–94 and 134–5, is a convincing counter to views put forward earlier by Lord Cooper and Professor Peter Stein.

25. Sir F. Pollock and F. W. Maitland, *History of English Law before the time of Edward I* 2nd ed. re-issued with an introduction by S. F. C. Milsom (Cambridge 1968) ii, 373. For a more recent assessment see C. Donahue, 'Roman Canon Law in the Medieval English Church: Stubbs vs. Maitland Re-examined' (1974) 72 *Michigan Law Review* 647–716.

26. *Registrum Monasterii de Passelet* (Maitland Club 1832; New Club 1877) pp. 165–7; and Cooper, *13th Century Cases* no. 22. See also Cosmo Innes, *Scotch Legal Antiquities* (Edinburgh 1872) 214–21.

27. Thomas Craig *Jus Feudale* trans. J. A. Clyde, 2 vols (Edinburgh and London 1934) I.3.24.

28. *Justiciary Cases 1624–1650* vol. 1, ed. Stair A. Gillon (Stair Society 1953) 121; and vol. 3, ed. J. Irvine Smith (Stair Society 1974) 690.

29.   Stair *Institutions of the Law of Scotland* ed. D. M. Walker (Edinburgh and Glasgow 1981) I.10.4.

30.   Stair *Institutions* I.10.7. It should be noted, however, that Scots law does recognise a category of obligations termed 'Obligationes Literis' for which there are certain requirements of form.

31.   *Maxwell v Gordon* (1775) Hailes' Reports (ed. Brown) 624 & 626.

32.   There is an outstanding modern biography of Elphinstone by Leslie Macfarlane: *William Elphinstone and the Kingdom of Scotland: 1431–1514* (Aberdeen 1985).

33.   R. C. van Caenegem, 'History of European Civil Procedure' *Encyclopedia of Comparative Law* vol. xvi, 2.19.

34.   Ollivant, *Court of the Official*; J. J. Robertson, 'Canon Law as a Source' [of Stair's *Institutions*] in *Stair Tercentenary Studies* ed. D. M. Walker (Stair Society 1981) 112–27, and 'Canon Law' in *The Laws of Scotland: Stair Memorial Encyclopedia* vol 25. paras 557–86.

35.   The Gulathing Code applied in south-west Norway, around Bergen, and west-over-sea in Iceland, the Faroes, Orkney and Shetland.

36.   On Udal law see now Jane Ryder, 'Udal Law', and Sir Thomas Smith's Editorial Excursus thereon in *Stair Memorial Encyclopaedia* vol 24, paras 301–16 and 317–29; also *Shetland Salmon Farmers Assn.* v *Crown Estate Commissioners* 1990 SCLR 484.

37.   *Acts of the Lords Auditors of Causes and Complaints* ed. T. Thomson (Edinburgh 1839) 21.

38.   Cooper, 'Dark Age of Scottish Legal History' *Selected Papers* 227.

39.   *Gibson's Trs* 1933 SC 190 & 198.

40.   Professor A. A. M. Duncan's 'The Central Courts before 1532' in *Introduction to Scottish Legal History* ed. G. C. H. Paton (Stair Society 1958) 321–40 is seminal, but his views on the significance of 1532 need to be revised in the light of Alan Harding, 'Medieval Brieves of Protection and the Development of the Common Law' 1966 *Juridical Review* 115–49; A. L. Murray, 'Sinclair's Practicks' in *Law-making and Law-makers* ed. Alan Harding (London 1980) 90–104; and H. L. MacQueen, 'Jurisdiction in Heritage and the Lords of Council and Session after 1532' in *Miscellany II* of the Stair Society. See also Sellar, 'Common Law of Scotland' (*supra* note 15).

41.   John Lesley or Leslie, *De Origine Moribus et rebus gestis Scotiae* in 16th century Scots translation, quoted in Peter Stein, 'Influence of Roman law on the Law of Scotland' 1963 *Juridical Review* 205–45 @ 216, reprinted in Peter Stein, *The Character and Influence of the Roman Civil Law* (London 1988) 319–59. For the influence of Roman law, see also Stein, 'Roman Law in Medieval Scotland' *Ius Romanum Medii Aevi* Pars V, 13b (Milan 1968) reprinted in Stein, *Character and Influence* 269–317; W. M. Gordon, 'Roman Law as a Source' [of Stair's *Institutions*] in *Stair Tercentenary Studies* 107–12; and 'Roman Law' in *Stair Memorial Encyclopaedia* vol. 25, paras 548–56.

42.   Cosmo Innes, *Scotch Legal Antiquities* 159.

43.   Cooper, 'Dark Age' *Selected Papers* 230.

44.   The Subscription of Deeds Acts are likely to be repealed shortly if the Scottish Law Commission's proposals for reform in this area are implemented.

45.   See particularly J. G. A. Pocock, *The Ancient Constitution and the Feudal Law* (Cambridge 1957; reissued with a retrospect, Cambridge 1987).

46.   Jenny Wormald, *Court, King and Community: Scotland 1470–1625* (London 1981) 181.

47.   Klaus Luig (trans. Sabine MacCormack), 'The Institutions of National Law in the 17th and 18th Centuries' 1972 *Juridical Review* 193–226.

48.   Balfour's *Practicks* circulated extensively in manuscript before the first printed edition of 1754. Balfour's *Practicks* and Hope's *Major Practicks* have both been reprinted this century by the Stair Society. It is pleasant to record that the present Lord President of the Court of Session, David Hope, is a direct descendant of Sir Thomas, via the 19th century Lord President Charles Hope of Granton.

49.   Cooper, *Scottish Legal Tradition* 9–10. (see also *infra* p. 69)

50.   See particularly *Stair Tercentenary Studies* ed. D. M. Walker (Stair Society 1981), and 'Stair Tercentenary Papers', being the second part of the *Juridical Review* for 1981.

51.   *Institutions* I.1.17 (1981 ed., p. 90).

52.   William M. Gordon, 'Stair's Use of Roman Law' in Harding, *Law-making and Law-makers* 120–6; *Jus Feudale* I.2.14.

53.   See particularly *The Jacobean Union: Six Tracts of 1604* edd. Bruce R. Galloway and

Brian P. Levack (Scottish History Society 1985), and Brian P. Levack, *The Formation of the British State: England, Scotland, and the Union 1603–1707* (Oxford 1987).

54. Article XVIII.

55. Article XIX.

56. A. J. MacLean, 'The 1707 Union: Scots Law and the House of Lords' (1983) 4 *Journal of Legal History* no. 3, 50–75; this issue was also printed as *New Perspectives in Scottish Legal History* edd. A. Kiralfy and Hector L. MacQueen (London 1984).

57. Article XXV.

58. A. V. Dicey, *The Law of the Constitution*, quoted in J. D. B. Mitchell, *Constitutional Law* (2nd ed. Edinburgh 1968) 19.

59. Mitchell, *Constitutional Law* chapters 4 and 5; and see pp. 98 and 69.

60. *MacCormick* v *Ld Advocate* 1953 SC 396 & 411. (See Appendix herein, p. 98.)

61. T. B. Smith, 'The Union of 1707 as Fundamental Law' 1957 *Public Law* 99–121, reprinted in T. B. Smith, *Studies Critical and Comparative* (Edinburgh 1962) 1–27, and Mitchell's *Constitutional Law* are crucial. A more recent contribution is Michael Upton, 'Marriage Vows of the Elephant: the Constitution of 1707' 1989 *Law Quarterly Review* 79–103.

62. Bruce Lenman, *The Jacobite Risings in Britain* (London 1980) 278.

63. There is a wealth of literature on the 'Scottish Enlightenment', including David Daiches, *The Scottish Enlightenment* (Saltire Society 1986). Adam Smith's *Lectures on Jurisprudence* are now in print, edited by R. L. Meek, D. D. Raphael and P. G. Stein (Oxford 1978). Dr John Cairns has recently begun to explore the relationship between the Enlightenment and legal education in Scotland in a series of articles.

64. Cooper, *Scottish Legal Tradition* 12. (See also *infra* p. 71.)

65. Ibid, 12. (See also *infra* p. 71.)

66. Ibid. 13. (See also *infra* p. 72.)

67. Ibid, 12. (See also *infra* p. 72.)

68. Ibid, 13. (See also *infra* p. 72.)

69. Ibid, 14. (See also *infra* p. 73.)

70. 1915 SC (HL) 52 @ 65.

71. (1858) 3 Macq 266 @ 285.

72. D. M. Walker, 'Bad Dreams Realised: The Consumer Credit Bill' 1974 *Scots Law Times (News)* 6–8 @ 8. The article is a remarkable example of sustained invective.

73. Cooper, *Scottish Legal Tradition* 15. (see also *infra* p. 74.)

I am deeply indebted to my colleague Dr Hector MacQueen for commenting on an earlier draft of this paper

W. DAVID H. SELLAR

Senior Lecturer in Scots Law at the University of Edinburgh

David Sellar is a Senior Lecturer in the Department of Scots Law at the University of Edinburgh. He has published extensively on the history of Scots law and on West Highland history and families. He is a Fellow of the Royal Historical Society and was from 1979 to 1984 Literary Director of the Stair Society.

The Scottish Legal Tradition

INTRODUCTION

For a lawyer to write about law for the benefit of laymen may not seem a very hopeful project, and it is certainly not an easy one. But one of the declared objects of the Saltire Society is to make Scotland conscious of her heritage; and of all the items which add up to make the sum total of that heritage none is more distinctive than Scotland's contribution to law. If the present series is to attain its purpose of disseminating knowledge of our record in order that this generation may draw inspiration from the past for further advances in the future, then assuredly it is impossible to dispense with a Pamphlet devoted to the Scottish Legal Tradition.

The reader need not be afraid of being immersed in the pages which follow in any detailed exposition of the technicalities of legal doctrine or practice. The aim is a different one. It is to outline some special characteristics of our system, and to indicate how it came into being, its peculiar excellences and defects, and the prospects for the future. It will of course be necessary to paint with a broad brush and to generalise widely, ignoring the qualifications and explanations which would be indispensable in a legal treatise, which this is not.

An inquiry on such lines should suggest fruitful ideas, for Scots Law is in a special sense the mirror of Scotland's history and traditions and a typical product of the national character, and it is just as truly a part of our national inheritance as our language or literature or religion. But the enquiry has more than a general cultural value. It has a present practical significance because it touches a matter which might at any time develop into a live political and social issue. This point requires a word of explanation.

If we exclude Russia, regarding which our information is still regrettably imperfect, two schools of legal thought have latterly been competing for the allegiance of the modern world—the Anglo-American and the Continental or Franco-German—the first founded upon English common law and equity and therefore predominantly inductive and empirical, and the second founded on the law of Rome and its modern offshoots in many recent codifications, and therefore predominantly systematic and deductive. Each of these schools can number its adherents in populations of hundreds of millions. Each has extended its sphere of influence far beyond the countries of its origin, initially as a result of conquest or colonisation, and latterly through voluntary adoption or imitation. Both systems are original: both can point to unbroken development from the distant past: and they are fundamentally different. Broadly speaking, every system of law now in use by the advanced civilisations of the present day belongs either to the one school or to the other, and the single effective choice which is available today to any state in search of a new code of law is to seek inspiration either in Anglo-American law or in Franco-German law. In every state, of course, the legal system always presents many local characteristics, and carries forward from its past a substantial element of national custom and tradition. But the moment we penetrate beneath the surface the dualism of modern law becomes unmistakable. It is as if the lawyers of the world spoke only in one or other of two languages and reasoned only in obedience to one or other of two methods of thought.

From this cosmic conflict in the field of law Scotland stands apart, content with a system of her own devising, which, as we shall see, now occupies a position somewhere midway between the two great opposing schools. And yet the citizens who look to Edinburgh for their supreme courts number only five millions. Scots Law has never been imposed, adopted or imitated *as a system* beyond the boundaries of Scotland. And when a Scot settles abroad, as so many do, he does not carry his native law with him.

In these remarkable circumstances the question which arises, and may at any time be pressed, is—how do we justify the retention in so small a country of an independent legal system? This Pamphlet may supply some material for an answer.

One further introductory caution may not be amiss. The lay reader who derives his impressions from the public press may be excused for imagining that the chief concern of the lawyer is with sensational murder trials and the latest regulations of the Ministry of Food. Similar misplaced emphasis would classify the works of Edgar Wallace and the Telephone Directory as masterpieces of English literature. A few hours spent in the Parliament House would correct such misconceptions. The law relating to murder and other major crimes is of considerable interest to practitioners in the Court of Justiciary—and to the accused—but it has little or no practical importance for the great mass of law-abiding citizens, and most lawyers contrive to lead a busy and useful professional life without once being involved in a *cause célèbre*. Similarly, we are all imprisoned in the network of modern departmental regulations, but these administrative directions have no better title to be recognised as an integral part of our system of jurisprudence than the current issue of the railway timetable. Accordingly, when we speak of a legal system let us think rather of the body of principles and doctrines which determine personal status and relations, which regulate the acquisition and enjoyment of property and its transfer between the living or its transmission from the dead, which define and control contractual and other obligations, and which provide for the enforcement of rights and the remedying of wrongs. These are the matters which inevitably touch the lives of all citizens at many points from the cradle to the grave, and their regulation is a function of government with which no civilised community can dispense and on the due administration of which the well-being of every society depends.

If you would know what a thing is, you must know how it came to be what it is: and if we are to acquire a just perspective for a brief survey of the modern law, we must consider first the pedigree of its leading doctrines. Let us therefore begin with the historical background.

THE HISTORICAL BACKGROUND

By contrast with the Anglo-American and Continental systems Scots Law is a comparative novelty. Though many of its roots extend far back into history, it is substantially true to say that our modern system of law only came into being in the later 17th century, and that it owed its birth to the synthetic genius of Viscount Stair, the author of our earliest institutional work, who fashioned out of a mass of partially digested raw material a coherent system of jurisprudence. For present purposes we cannot ignore pre-Stair law, but we need not linger beside it.

When Scots Law first emerges above the horizons of reliable history in the 12th and 13th centuries, it is in the main Anglo-Norman law—with a difference. These were the days when England led the world of law, and it was only natural that under the prevalent Norman influences

Scotland should borrow from England many of the ingenious and novel institutions and devices which were being successfully tried out in the South; and these were superimposed upon a stratum of local customary law and a certain amount of Canon and Roman law, which we owed to the ubiquitous and omnicompetent ecclesiastical organisation of Innocent III and his successors. But there was no slavish copying. Even in those early days the Scottish mind evidently recoiled from excessive intricacy and artificiality, such as disfigured the English Law of Edward I, and it was not a case of wholesale and indiscriminate borrowing but of critical picking and choosing, simplifying, adapting and rationalising. Before the end of the 13th century Scots Law and English Law were already recognisably different, though bearing many marks of close relationship.

Then came the Wars of Independence, the greatest line of cleavage in all Scottish history, and the initial phase of Scottish legal development came to an abrupt end. We carried forward from the initial phase into the later law something of the grammar and even the idiom of Roman and Canon Law and not a little local custom, but of English Law not a trace. Of course Feudal Law persisted (and persists to this day) but it was not in England that Feudalism was invented. For four hundred years Scots lawyers resolutely turned their backs upon England and English Law; and the law students from Scotland who had begun to flock to the University of Oxford later found in Bologna and Pisa, then in Paris and Orleans, and finally in Leyden and Utrecht, a more congenial atmosphere for study and a powerful source of inspiration for constructive work.

The political strife and economic troubles of the 14th and 15th centuries were hardly compatible with the development of private law, and this is the Dark Age of our legal history, only fitfully illuminated by a number of remarkable 'statutes,' which are still pivots of our law and which show that, despite the difficulties of their task, the lawyers had never laid their work aside. In process of time the French alliance and the steady pressure of Continental influences bore fruit in the gradual incorporation into Scots Law of a great mass of the Roman law as taught by the French and Dutch civilians, which made an irresistible appeal to the Scottish mind. Once again the appropriation was not indiscriminate but carefully selective, the choice being confined to broad principles and praetorian equity, by recourse to which the gaps in our infant philosophy of law were repaired and its imperfections cured.

With the establishment of the Court of Session in 1532 the stage seemed to be set for an immediate and notable legal advance, but the religious and political controversies of the 16th and early 17th centuries were unpropitious for the arts of peace and distracted the lawyers from their long-term programme. Remarkable developments took place in certain directions, especially in relation to the land laws, but on the whole the advance was haphazard and unsystematic. In the Commonwealth period there occurred a complete but temporary break in Scottish legal administration when the Court of Session was superseded for some years by Cromwell's nominees. But when the 'English Judges' disappeared at the Restoration, their work and influence vanished with them, and the broken threads were picked up and united once again.

Then came Stair. The publication of his *Institutions* in 1681 marked the creation of Scots Law as we have since known it—an original amalgam of Roman Law, Feudal Law and native customary law, systematised by resort to the law of nature and the Bible, and illuminated by many flashes of ideal metaphysic. To this work and its author every Scots lawyer has since paid a tribute of almost superstitious reverence, and the resort still occasionally made to Stair in the House of Lords and the Privy Council suggests that it is not only in the estimation of his fellow-countrymen that he falls to be ranked amongst the great jurists of all time.

Throughout the 18th century development proceeded at a steadily increasing pace with continued reliance upon the law of Rome and with a revival of interest in Feudal law as a consequence of the forfeitures and redistribution of lands following upon the Jacobite rebellions. The position was strongly consolidated by the posthumous publication in 1773 of the second of our great institutional works, Erskine's *Institute*— not an original creation like Stair's unique work, but a comprehensive re-statement of the law of unchallenged authority, descriptive of the system as it had developed to meet the changed circumstances of the writer's age.

Meantime commerce had come to occupy a more important place in the affairs of men, and the international contacts to which it gave rise attracted increasing attention to the Law Merchant as it was being developed in England and elsewhere. For the third time in three successive centuries a Scottish jurist of world fame was ready to supply the need, and with the appearance early in the 19th century of his *Commentaries* and *Principles* George Joseph Bell took his well-merited place alongside Stair and Erskine as the third member of the Scottish legal trinity.

Let us pause to single out some salient features of this abbreviated retrospect.

(1) For long the story of Scots Law is simply a record of false starts and rejected experiments. This was not the fault of our lawyers but their misfortune, for the interruptions in their work were due to the disasters which successively overwhelmed their country, and their successive changes of outlook faithfully reflect the vicissitudes of their distracted fellow-citizens.

(2) Throughout the bulk of the formative period Scotland was too small and her executive government was far too weak to admit of the evolution of an entirely original legal system. There has never been much in Scots Law which is indigenous to Scotland. Our lawmakers wisely preferred to exercise their originality in selecting what they thought best in the systems which they saw around them and in avoiding the mistakes into which they considered that other systems had fallen. Twice over—first in the 13th and then in the 17th century—Scotland constructed a legal system out of imported ideas, and on both occasions the work was done with a sturdy independence of outlook. From first to last the effort was to attain simplicity, flexibility and directness, and to attain these things systematically.

(3) The Fates, who so relentlessly deferred and frustrated the construction of our legal system, and even despoiled us of our legal records—once by the hands of Edward I and a second time by the hands of Oliver Cromwell—made handsome reparation when they eventually sent us the three jurists whose masterpieces have done so much to create and to preserve the rational simplicity of Scots Law.

(4) In the 18th century Scots Law came within an ace of sinking its identity in the Franco-German school, and only failed to do so because of the growing power of the political forces introduced by the Union of 1707. To this day our legal affinities are markedly closer with this school than with Anglo-American law, though we have latterly moved—or drifted—to an intermediate position.

It has been well said that the fabric of mature Scots Law is as variegated as a tartan. But it is possible to overstress the vicissitudes though which our law has passed and the lack of real continuity in its development. The forgotten architects of our system, who toiled over a heart-breaking task for hundreds of years, were all possessed of the same qualities—self-reliant, severely practical, invincibly logical and with a metaphysical bent—and they had something within them correspondent to the spirit of the supreme achievements of Roman jurisprudence. When at long last they had completed their task in the early 19th century, they had furnished Scotland with what most comparative lawyers will agree was an admirably finished philosophical system, well in advance of its times. That result was attained by the persevering application of the same technique—the contriving of the fewest possible number of tools capable of performing the largest possible number of different jobs, and the deduction of the widest possible range of consequences from the smallest possible number of carefully chosen general principles. These men may not have been creative artists in law, but they were supremely successful craftsmen.

THE PRESENT POSITION [1949]

It was of set purpose that in our historical survey the line was drawn about 1820. That may seem a long time ago, but the purpose of history is not to chronicle events but to isolate and interpret controlling tendencies; and we are still too near the trees of the 19th century to see the wood. In law the last one hundred and twenty years belong to the dynamic present rather than to the historic past.

It is now convenient to introduce one technical term, beloved of British lawyers, and used by them in so many different senses as sorely to mystify the Continental school of jurisprudence—the common law. Let us define it as meaning the whole of our legal rules and doctrines which are not derived from enactments of the United Kingdom Parliament. In this sense the great bulk of the law of Scotland in 1820 was common law, owing its origin to Roman Law, Feudal Law and ancient customs, as developed, interpreted and applied by the Courts and expounded by the institutional writers. The first leading characteristic of the period since 1820 has been the steady encroachment of modern statute upon the common law, mainly as the fruit of conscious efforts at law reform, but sometimes as the by-product of political and social theory. The formidable and still rising torrent of acts, regulations and, orders has been the subject of many an unavailing protest by lawyers and laymen alike, and the rule to which we still pay lip service that every citizen is presumed to know the law has long since

71

degenerated into a pious fiction. Indeed there are now vast tracts of so-called 'law' the mastery of each of which is the lifework of a specialist—Income Tax, Social Insurance, Local Government and many others—and, although the interpretation and application of the positive rules which deal with such matters now engage much of the time and attention of the Courts, none of them contains more than a faint tincture of juristic principle. The attitude of the normal lawyer to the provisions which define and regulate these sub-legal matters is that of the mathematician to the table of logarithms. He consults them when required, and then dismisses them from his mind. The important point for the layman to grasp is that, despite this enormous accretion of the indispensable apparatus of the complicated modern state, it is still the common law of Scotland that regulates and defines all the main rights and duties of the Scottish citizen. In 1948 as in 1820 the great bulk of the law of Scotland is still common law—improved, simplified and modified in details, but in essence the same.

The second leading characteristic of the period since 1820 has been the revival of English influence, not as in the 13th century through the conscious pursuit by Scots lawyers of a desirable foreign contact, but unsought and indirect. It has made itself felt increasingly through two different channels, each of which merits examination.

The first is the legislative practice adopted at Westminster through pressure of work whereby statutes are normally drafted by English lawyers for England, and then applied with the minimum of 'adaptation' to Scotland, the tacit assumption being that whatever England wants must be good enough for Scotland, and that statutes should always conform as closely as possible to a uniform pattern, capable of being understood and applied from London by one set of officials. In the purely administrative and governmental sphere this legislative technique is an intelligible consequence of the political union between the two countries, and often does no harm. But in the last fifty years the statute book will reveal not a few instances of the forcible compression of Scottish legal principles into English moulds without much regard for the resulting strains and distortions. Every translator knows that there are many terms in one language which have no exact equivalent in another; and what is true of language is also true of law.

The second channel of English influence is the House of Lords, the final court of appeal for Scotland in civil (but not in criminal) cases. We are habituated in these islands to constitutional usages which defy logical justification but which nevertheless work; and that is probably why we see nothing anomalous in confiding the last word on a Roman system of law to a court whose members are drawn predominantly from the opposite camp of Anglo-American law. As was observed of Newman's conversion, the matter has been apologised for but never explained. No difficulty arises when the case relates, as so many appeals do, to some problem in fiscal or other modern legislation common to the United Kingdom. But when the matter in issue is some narrowly balanced problem of Scots common law, it is only natural that an English lawyer's search for a solution should be from the angle of English common law and equity and that his logical processes should be inductive and empirical. As a result it has happened that there have been authoritatively imposed upon our common law more than one complete innovation for which Scottish lawyers have not been enthusiastic in their acknowledgements, and one of which has recently had to be excised by the surgical operation of an amending act. Even in our own courts cases have occurred to which our own law provided no explicit answer but English law did, or appeared to do; and in such cases it is very tempting to adopt the ready-made English solution and to justify the adoption by the assertion that in regard to the matter in hand the two systems are the same. They rarely are. The resemblance is usually superficial.

The academic lawyers of many countries are widely discussing today the ideal of the eventual fusion of the Roman and the Anglo-American schools of legal thought in a super-system, so rational in its conceptions and so compelling in its equity as to command universal assent. Such an ideal, assuming it to be desirable and practicable, would be better achieved by mutual co-operation between the two schools in a systematic attack upon the problem and in an effort to reconcile deduction and empiricism rather than by the haphazard inoculation of one system with ideas taken from another.

Be that as it may, the fact is that Scots Law and English Law are today much closer to each other than when Bell wrote his *Principles*, and Scots Law has correspondingly drifted further away from the Continental school of thought. The traffic in ideas between Scotland and England has not been one-way traffic, for England has recently incorporated in her system a good deal that Scotland already possessed. The two outstanding matters in regard to which Scotland has latterly followed the English, and rejected the Continental, tradition are: (i) in adopting, almost unconsciously, the English rule of the rigidly binding force of judicial precedents, and (ii) in rejecting large-scale codification, now almost invariable outside the Anglo-American camp, and leaving her common law as judge-made law. These things are now second nature to us, but they represent a significant departure from the Scottish tradition, and they still excite the comment of jurists of the Continental school. Codification, or something very like it, has of course been undertaken in special branches of modern mercantile law which transcends national boundaries; but our old common law is still uncodified and likely to remain so, though Bell demonstrated long ago how it might be done.

But the anchors of the common law of Scotland have not yet dragged. We still retain, and are justified in retaining, in their pristine purity the mass of our classical principles. There are two special matters in respect of which we have always differed from Anglo-American law, (i) in refusing to admit any distinction whatever between law and equity, and in having from the first merged the Chancery and the Common Law Courts in one; and (ii) in subordinating the remedy to the right, and attaching no importance or value to forms of action as such. These distinctions may seem of small significance to a layman, and they are certainly much less important today than they were a generation or two ago. But they still vitally affect the processes of thought by which a Scots and an English lawyer respectively attack a legal problem, and the lines of approach adopted by the two systems in expanding and developing the law to meet the changing needs of a changing society.

Every allowance must be made for the partialities and prejudices created in every lawyer in the course of a professional lifetime devoted to the study and application of any one system; but this assertion may be ventured that, tested by the standards of the modern philosophy of jurisprudence and by experience, the classical law of Stair, Erskine and Bell has proved to be eminently suited to Scottish needs and eminently capable of adaptation and adjustment to solve the new problems of a transformed social world, which its authors never beheld even in a vision.

Let us now descend from generalities to particulars by passing in review a few of the distinctive features of Scots Law. The limits imposed by this short study demand that this review should be highly selective; but the broad outlines of the complete picture will sufficiently appear from a glance at the law of the family, the land laws, the law of

74

succession, the law of contract, the law of reparation, the civil courts and procedure, and our system of criminal law and administration.

It is a painful confession to have to make, but all that follows is Lowland and not Highland law. The story of the clan system and its incidents, which persisted so late in Scotland's history, and of such special topics as the Udal Law of the Orkneys and Zetland, is outside the limits of any brief account of Scots Law, the harvest of which was gathered below the 500 foot contour line, and mainly south of the Forth.

The Law of the Family

Marriage, divorce and the personal and property relations of husband and wife and of parent and child are common to all civilised societies, and the differences between one legal system and another, or between different ages of the same system, tend to be superficial. In Scotland, the basis of our law is immemorial custom and the religious tradition, considerably coloured by Canonist doctrine, traces of which still survive.

Until a few years ago Scots Law was unusual in allowing marriage to be constituted without either official formality or sacerdotal benediction. The old 'irregular' Scottish marriage provided material for juristic disquisitions and plots for novels, written by authors who fondly imagined that it was not uncommon in Scotland for marriages to be contracted inadvertently and even unawares. But it was only when the abuse of the irregular marriage and its commercialisation at Gretna Green and elsewhere led to instances of hardship and complications in the vital statistics that it was deemed advisable to sweep it away. There were no mourners at the graveside. But it would be quite wrong to suppose that this change made much, if any, difference to the vast majority of prospective spouses, for a very large proportion of irregular marriages were immediately registered under a sheriff's warrant, the need for proof of married status being nowadays so vital for the purposes of many insurance and other official schemes. The alteration in the law has thus meant nothing to those who prefer a civil to a religious marriage except the substitution of a registrar for a sheriff as the functionary representing the interests of the state.

Some ten years ago England introduced far-reaching reforms in her law of divorce, and Scotland took advantage of the opportunity to make a few minor changes, the most notable being the introduction of divorce for insanity. The English controversy chiefly centred around divorce for desertion: but Scotland has had divorce for desertion since 1573, and numerous Scottish decisions have refined and developed every aspect of this difficult remedy. Scotland has never known the provisional decree *nisi* of English divorce practice.

Our law of parent and child has been slightly modified by modern legislation dealing with child welfare and related topics, but in the main our common law principles still stand and work well. We still adhere to the Roman tradition of drawing a dividing line at puberty between the pupil and the minor instead of adopting the English rule of classifying all who are not adult as infants. An anomalous inroad upon the common law was recently effected by the introduction of the institution of adoption, the merits or demerits of which are still an open question.

It is possible that future transformations of social habits and religious outlook may be reflected in a demand for changes in this chapter of our law; but short of that no substantial alterations seem either probable or desirable. The standard treatises of the late Lord Fraser and the steady current of decisions on fresh aspects of old questions will supply our needs for a long time to come.

The Land Laws

This is the branch of Scots Law which is most distinctively Scottish and which has been allowed to evolve without the intrusion of alien influence for some eight hundred years. Though the law has been simplified and clarified by amending statutes again and again, its central doctrines are still purely feudal, and, so far as known, it is at present the most feudal of any system of land laws in the world. This is at once its peculiar merit and its defect.

In the 17th and 18th centuries, and even earlier, our classical system of conveyancing and heritable rights was worked out to the last detail with a rigorous logic and a felicitous ingenuity which it is a pleasure to study. The great Scottish lawyers of these days were pre-eminently feudalists, and lavished their acumen and sagacity for generations on the task of perfecting the Scottish version of feudal practice. The law came to pivot upon the public registration of deeds, and with the establishment in the 17th century (after much trial and error) of the Register of Sasines, substantially in the form in which it still exists, Scotland was recognised as having equipped herself with a very advanced code of land laws which for long was discussed with envy and admiration by the lawyers of foreign states. There were few of the innumerable problems which cropped up before the middle of the 19th century which proved incapable of elegant solution by application of, or deduction from, the finished principles which had been elaborated by the old feudalists, and the leading cases of the period contain many judgments which are models of philosophic law.

All this may be put to the credit side of the account, and an impressive total it makes. But there is also a debit side, and it has been steadily mounting. Lawyers still living had to learn in their youth much medieval lore about antiquated incidents of tenure, which still occasionally stir in their graves to the extreme discomfiture of the younger school; for it is no disparagement to the present generation of Scots lawyers to say that Lord Dunedin was the last of the feudalists. A great deal of dead wood has been pruned away by the later conveyancing statutes, but a great deal still remains, and it is to be feared that we have lived a little too long upon our feudal reputation and have hardly kept abreast of a new world to which the very idea of vassalage, however theoretical, is repellent.

For instance, it is both easier and cheaper to acquire a marketable title to a Rolls Royce than to a shed in which to keep it, and much simpler to invest £100,000 in Stock Exchange shares or securities than £100 on a heritable bond. The preparation of deeds relating to land is the province of skilled experts, and the same is true of the examination of title deeds and the searching of the official records: and every time a property changes hands the whole process may have to be undertaken anew. Meantime younger countries in Europe and America, unencumbered by long tradition and able to start with a more or less clean slate, have set up various types of registration of title by means of which rights to land can be transferred at trifling cost, usually with a state guarantee of the title, which is investigated once and for all under official auspices. In an old country like Scotland a change-over from the old to a new system would be far from easy, and there are many incidental complications arising from our local law of property—a notable example being the wide prevalence in Scottish burghs of tenements, subdivided both vertically and horizontally into separate premises, each of which is, or is capable of being, owned in fee simple by a different proprietor, who further enjoys a common interest along with his fellow-proprietors in the remainder of the building. To delineate such rights on a map or plan would tax the skill of any draftsman, and their compendious description on a card-index might be very difficult. Whether the administrative changes required to give Scotland a modern system of registration of title would be feasible, and how far it might be necessary to preface them by recasting our land laws as England did by the Birkenhead reforms of twenty years ago, are large questions to which a Committee presided over by Lord Macmillan is at present seeking an answer. The problems are not new and drastic answers have been proposed in the past: for it is on record that an iconoclastic Lord Advocate once drafted a one-clause Bill with the single provision: 'The Feudal System is hereby abolished'!

Scotland is rich in her legal literature relating to heritable rights, beginning with Craig's historic *De Feudis* and extending downwards through a long succession of valuable treatises and published lectures, written by feudalists and modern conveyancers of high authority. We need these works; for the many conveyancing statutes have never been codified, and it is still on occasions necessary for the conveyancer to know not only what the law now is but what it was at some date in the past.

The Law of Succession

The rules which in Scotland regulate the transmission of property from the dead to the living, whether by will or on intestacy, have not been deeply affected by statute, their chief continuing source being Roman Law, Canon Law and native customary law, now heavily overlaid and refined by an embarrassingly large mass of decisions.

The basic principles of the law of wills, trusts and settlements of all kinds are adequate and distinct; but it is impossible to set a limit to the speculative benevolence of testators or to the ingenuity or wrong-headedness of their advisers, with the result that the stream of litigation shows little signs of abating. The title of 'Succession' is still much the largest in our digests of cases, and no branch of our law reveals narrower distinctions or more subtle refinements of interpretation. This is probably inevitable, and the difficulty is by no means confined to Scotland. But it is always a pity to have to credit ordinary people with metaphysical conceptions which it is certain that they never harboured, and which they were probably quite incapable of apprehending. No lawyer would relish the task of expounding to an intelligent layman the doctrine of 'vesting subject to defeasance'.

A distinctive and salutary rule of Scots Law which dates from the earliest times is that which prohibits a husband (and latterly a wife) from disinheriting his (or her) spouse, and a parent from disinheriting his children, by guaranteeing to the surviving spouse or children certain 'legal rights' in the estate of the deceased. Another speciality of our law is the acceptance as sufficiently authenticated of the 'holograph' will, written in the testator's own hand and signed by him but without further solemnities of execution. We have also elaborated through long tracts of decisions a variety of canons of interpretation, dealing with the effect to be assigned to the expressions most commonly used in testamentary documents, and the consequences to be attributed to common contingencies, such as the birth of a child to a testator after the execution of his will, or the predecease of a legatee leaving issue. On the whole, and for all its unavoidable elaboration, our law of testate succession works well, and the capacity of its foundation doctrines for expansion and adaptation is by no means exhausted.

When we pass from testate to intestate succession any cause for complacency vanishes. Our rules are redolent of the 18th century when land and interests in land were the wealth of the community. This is pre-eminently the chapter of our law which cries aloud to be re-written, for it is out of touch with present-day realities and ought to be discarded as obsolete and outworn. No sane testator would dream of making the distribution of his estate which, if he dies without making a will, our law will make for him. Twenty years ago the Birkenhead reforms in England effected the corresponding changes in the law which were required there, and a like reform in Scotland is long overdue. Proposals to that end, mooted before the last war, were deferred as a result of the international situation, but they are bound to be revived, and the sooner, the better.

In addition to the institutional writers and a huge corpus of decisions we are well served in this branch of our law by Lord McLaren's monumental treatise on *Wills and Succession* and by a number of valuable modern textbooks. But it is on our decisions that we chiefly rely.

The Law of Contract

Many chapters of the law of contract which specially affect the mercantile community—charter-parties, bills of lading, bills of exchange, sale of goods and marine insurance, for example—have largely passed from the control of individual national systems of law and in the main are now international in character. Local features still persist, but future development in this field is likely to be a matter for international convention. It is with the general law of contract that we are now concerned, and this is a subject which has been successfully developed in Scots Law on Roman foundations and in general conformity to the Franco-German pattern. Without breach of the initial promise not to enter into technical details it would be impossible to discuss the features which differentiate Scots Law from Anglo-American, but it may be permissible to observe that the cardinal English doctrine of 'consideration', which so deeply affects their law of contract, has no part in Scots Law, and that in recent times the tendency has been for English Law to be brought into conformity with the principles which have long prevailed in Scotland and which originated in Roman Law.

The reader may be surprised at this repeated invocation of Roman Law, but it requires no apology. In certain types of human enterprise, of which the formation of obligations is one, the essence of the transaction—the intention of parties, their mutual consent, the factors which may exclude such consent, and many other elements—has stood, and must continue to stand, unaltered through the ages. In relation to such matters the conclusions wrought out by generations of jurists, belonging to a race whose genius for jurisprudence is unexampled in history, are imperishable, incapable of being abolished, and in many respects incapable of being improved upon. Their collective wisdom has furnished the groundwork for the municipal law for half the world, and it is not from blind traditionalism, but from recognition of the supreme merits of its model, that the Scots Law of Contract has always been, and will remain, Roman in principle.

Our chief authority on the law of contract is George Joseph Bell, along with whose famous works it is not wholly inappropriate to mention the outstanding modern treatise of the late Professor Gloag of Glasgow University.

The Law of Reparation

What the Scots lawyer calls a 'delict' and the English lawyer a 'tort' might be popularly defined as an actionable wrong for which the common remedy is an award of damages. Its categories are already legion, and they continue to expand in numbers and variety. The subject is hardly known to early law: it was confined within narrow limits when our institutional writers lived and worked; and it has only been within the last two generations that the full flood has burst upon us.

On this topic (as on nearly every other) Scots Law was true to type by laying down, while the subject was still fluid and adaptable, a few cardinal principles from which a very wide range of consequences could be deduced. Chief amongst these was the principle that liability for reparation cannot exist without fault or breach of duty—a rule which stands in vivid contrast to the original basis in principle of the English law of tort, which imposed liability in many cases where there was no fault. In more recent times this point and other vital distinctions in principle have been progressively obscured in the wilderness of single instances, and in certain restricted but important types of case the indiscriminate citation of English precedents in Scottish cases and the facile assumption that the law must be the same on both sides of the Border have threatened to produce in Scotland rather unsystematic and illogical results. The law both here and in England is still in active development, and with no strong lead from our institutional writers and with the Anglo-American influence at its highest, it is to be feared that in process of time the rational simplicity of our law of delict will be submerged,—not because it is inferior to, but because it is different from, English Law.

The subject is one on which in every country new problems are presenting themselves for solution every day. In the last resort it does not greatly matter what solutions are found, but it does greatly matter that in any given country the law should develop systematically and logically so that its future trend and application shall be capable of reasoned forecast. Either oil or water is preferable to the unsatisfactory emulsion which results from attempts to mix the two.

Civil Courts and Procedure

The Supreme Court, which sits in Edinburgh, consists of the Lord President, the Lord Justice-Clerk, and twelve Senators of the College of Justice, and is divided into the Inner and the Outer House. The Inner House deals with appeals from the Outer House and from inferior courts, and also exercises an original jurisdiction in a number of special types of case. It sits in two Divisions, the full complement of each being four, the First Division presided over by the Lord President and the Second by the Lord Justice-Clerk. Owing to the demands of criminal circuits and other special duties, the services of Division judges are frequently required elsewhere, and the Divisions often sit with their minimum quorum of three judges. The Outer House consists of the remaining six judges each of whom sits alone as a judge of first instance. When, exceptionally, issues of high principle and difficulty are raised involving the consideration of conflicting authorities, the two Divisions may sit together as a Court of Seven Judges with authority to overrule prior Division judgments; and still more exceptionally a case can be referred to the Whole Court. In these expedients Scotland retains the last safeguard against the excessive rigidity of precedent. Normally the decisions of each Division are binding on both, and on the Outer House and inferior courts. Considerations of convenience lead to the appropriation of some types to one Division or to one Outer House Judge; but every judge is assumedly capable of dealing with every type of case, and there is no subdivision of the Court as in England into branches, each dealing only with specified classes of judicial work.

Throughout the whole of Scotland from Shetland to Wigtown there are distributed some fifty locally resident Sheriff-Substitutes who are full-time professional judges, roughly corresponding to the English County Court judge, but with a wider civil jurisdiction and extensive criminal duties. The sheriff as a judicial and administrative officer dates from the 12th century and is thus much older than the Court of Session, and by reason of the multiplicity of his functions he has always occupied a very important place in the Scottish governmental scheme. In civil cases an appeal lies from the Sheriff Substitute either to the Sheriff Principal, of whom there are now twelve, or to the Court of Session; and there is also an appeal from the Sheriff Principal to the Court of Session. In criminal cases, the Sheriff in Scotland discharges the great bulk of the work which in England is entrusted to lay justices in petty or quarter sessions; for the Justice of the Peace is not indigenous to Scotland but is a comparatively late importation, and he has never played more than a very minor part in the judicial administration of Scotland and in many parts of the country does not function judicially at all.

The procedure of the Court of Session was overhauled in 1934, and minor improvements were effected in the present year. It retains of set purpose a special feature which has characterised its written pleadings for centuries, *viz.*, the requirement that the essential facts underlying both the demand for a remedy and the defence to that demand should be sufficiently set out in an articulate 'condescendence', and that the legal basis of both the claim and the defence should be formulated in a series of 'pleas in law' or legal propositions related to the facts set out. When the pleadings have been adjusted, the case in fact and in law advanced for both the parties is, or ought to be, instantly discoverable. Neither will be allowed at any later stage to trespass beyond the limits of their adjusted pleadings, and if the facts averred provide an insufficient legal basis for the claim or the defence, the action or the defences may be dismissed as 'irrelevant' without further enquiry—a procedure analogous to the now discredited English 'demurrer'. Great value is attached in Scotland to this method of written pleading, which compels the parties at the initial stages of a litigation to define with precision the essence of their case, and which enables many a case to be disposed of cheaply and quickly without the expense and delay involved in an investigation into the facts. Lest it should be supposed that Scottish lawyers are unreasonably prejudiced in favour of their native methods, it is worth recording that, when the United States Government was engaged in 1912 in drafting what became the Federal Equity Rules, they applied for advice to Lord Chancellor Loreburn, who suggested that it would be worth their while to consider the Scottish method of pleading 'which in my opinion is the best'. Coming from so authoritative and independent a source, this is indeed high praise.

Trial by jury in civil cases has had a curious history in Scotland. When the early Anglo-Norman influence had evaporated, the civil jury disappeared from our midst and had been completely forgotten long before the early years of the 19th century when it was re-introduced from England. For long it did not work well, and there was much controversy on the question what types of case were, and what were not, appropriate for trial by jury. Gradually we became habituated to the innovation but are not yet resigned to its acceptance. Numerically the vast majority of jury trials now relate to traffic accidents, and the institution has become an accessory of the internal combustion engine. It has never been explained why twelve casually chosen ladies and gentlemen should be assumed to be better qualified to determine whether John Smith sounded his horn or passed a traffic signal 'on the red' than a highly trained judge, familiar with the rules of evidence and accustomed to its appraisal. Moreover as all civil jury trials take place in the Court of Session, what we enjoy in Scotland is not trial by jury but trial by Edinburgh citizens. For six years during the recent war jury trials in civil cases were suspended, and the work was taken by the judges in their stride. But now jury trials are back again. These facts are worth pondering by those who justify the civil jury in Scotland by a vague and mistaken reference to Magna Carta or the Treaty of Union. At a time of such economic difficulty it is odd that we can tolerate the waste of manpower involved in taking so many people from their work, often for days at a time, in order that they may settle the quarrels of other people.

This part of the picture would be incomplete without a word regarding the organisation of the legal profession. The solicitors have formed a large number of central and local societies, recently loosely federated under a General Council, the premier society being that of the Writers to the Signet. There is nothing corresponding to the Inns of Court, but the Faculty of Advocates is a corporation of historic dignity with an amazing record of public service and a unique cultural tradition, its members having included during the last two hundred years the majority of the outstanding figures in the Scottish annals of law, literature and public life.

Criminal Law and Administration

This is a branch of our legal system in which Scotland may justly take pride, and which has been maintained at a high pitch of efficiency. The substantive criminal law is indigenous to Scotland, and it is almost entirely common law with only trifling statutory ingredients. In the main it is the product of native custom, elaborated and developed by judicial decision; and in this respect it enjoys a flexibility and a capacity for expansion which are denied to many countries, of which England is one, in which nearly every crime or offence has to be found in the provisions of a statute. Scotland has been fortunate in a succession of notable treatises on the law of crime, commencing with the famous *Commentaries* of Baron David Hume, published in 1797, which has all but attained the dignity of an institutional work, and richly merits the high authority in which it is held.

Whatever the position may have been in days gone by—and if Scotland had her Braxfield, England had her Jeffreys—the Scottish law of crime and especially of criminal evidence has latterly been

84

exceedingly scrupulous in guaranteeing fairness to the accused, preferring to allow the guilty to escape rather than incur any risk of convicting the innocent. Notable instances of this attitude are afforded by our refusal of an opening statement to the prosecutor and our concession to the accused of the last word to the jury; by the very sparing admissions of confessions or incriminating statements by the accused; and by the cardinal rule that, (apart from a few statutory exceptions), no person can be convicted unless there is evidence of at least two witnesses implicating the accused in the commission of the crime charged. The chief search in most prosecutions is thus for sufficient corroboration, in the absence of which a conviction cannot take place, or, if obtained, cannot stand, however credible the principal witness may be.

Another outstanding feature of our criminal law is the exclusion of private prosecutions, and the concentration in the hands of the Lord Advocate, acting through his Deputies in the Crown Office, and his local officers in each sheriffdom, (the procurators fiscal), of the sole right to prosecute all crimes, exclusive of petty offences which are dealt with in police and minor courts. By this method Scotland avoids the prejudicial publicity in the earlier stages of a criminal prosecution which arises from coroner's inquests and proceedings before magistrates, and secures that the jurors empanelled to try an accused person know substantially nothing of the case until they hear the evidence from the lips of the witnesses at the actual trial. This feature of our system, which involves that all preliminary enquiries are conducted officially and confidentially, has worked extremely well, and, notwithstanding the very wide discretion which is vested in the Lord Advocate, it is over a century since a holder of that high office has been publicly called in question on the charge of abusing his powers. It is another prerogative of the Lord Advocate that he, and he alone, determines by his estimate of the gravity of the alleged crime, whether the prosecution shall take place in the High Court with a jury, or in the Sheriff Court with a jury, or before a sheriff sitting without a jury. The sheriff's powers of imposing punishment are limited, and major cases cannot be taken in the sheriff court; but once a case has been sent to a sheriff to be tried summarily without a jury, the accused has no right to demand a jury.

Since 1926 Scotland has had a Court of Criminal Appeal from which no appeal lies to the House of Lords, so that in the whole field of criminal administration Scotland still enjoys self-determination. Our native principles have served us well and have proved capable in more than one recent decision of being expanded to cover situations of a novel type. The process of detailed improvement of the law and the procedure to meet new needs is constantly in progress; but taken as a whole this branch of our law is one with which the Scottish people may feel well satisfied, and which will challenge comparison with any criminal system in the world.

The Lord President of the Court of Session, the Lord Justice-Clerk and the remaining Senators of the College of Justice occupy automatically the positions of Lord Justice General, Lord Justice-Clerk and Lords Commissioners of Justiciary; and wearing different robes, conduct the major trials not only in Edinburgh but in various Circuit towns in Scotland, and dispose of the criminal appeals in Edinburgh.

In conclusion mention should be made of a feature of our criminal law which attracts more public notice than it deserves—the verdict of Not Proven. Historically the Not Proven verdict is an accident, if not a mistake. Logically it may be difficult to justify. Practically, it works, and its abolition might have unintended consequences. However plainly a presiding judge may explain that an accused is presumed to be innocent until he is proved guilty, that he is entitled to the benefit of every reasonable doubt, and that the burden of proof is on the prosecution, the hard-headed Scots juror will nevertheless draw a common-sense distinction between the person who is entitled to leave the Court without a stain on his character, and the person whose guilt is beyond moral doubt but who luckily escapes by the skin of his teeth for lack of some element of corroboration, or on some other narrow ground. The question is an open one, but those who complain of the stigma supposed to attach to an acquittal on a Not Proven verdict should consider whether, if there were no such verdict, the result in a narrow case might be not an acquittal but a conviction. There are occasions when sheer logic may not be the safest guide. It only remains to add that we accept a verdict by a majority and do not insist on unanimity; and long experience has not given rise to any demand for a change, either from the public or from the legal profession.

THE PROSPECTS FOR THE FUTURE

The safest method of supplying the contents of this section would be to leave a blank page. But this is no time to play for safety. Let us ignore the enigmas of the present situation and endeavour to apply with courage and cool detachment the lessons to be learnt from the preceding pages.

The Scottish legal tradition is a thing to be prized both in Scotland and beyond its Borders, and the public of Scotland should be more conscious of the fact. It is in a very real sense a typical product of the Scottish ethos, and has attracted to its enthusiastic service some of the greatest figures in our country's history. There are not many legal systems which can number amongst their modern exponents three such universally respected lawyers as Lord President Inglis, Lord Watson and Lord Dunedin, whose work is known the world over. We need not be afraid to submit Scots Law to the scrutiny of comparative jurists or to the test of its capacity to meet present-day needs. As has been shown, there are certain parts which are due for reconditioning and overhaul, having worn out through long service; but there is no legal system of which the like cannot be said, and against the deficiencies we can set many conspicuous successes. But it is possible to go further and to consider Scots Law from a wider standpoint than the merely local and domestic. In respect of the intermediate position which it now occupies between the two great schools of legal thought, Scots Law is at the moment unique. A very eminent and detached critic, Professor Levy Ullmann of Paris, has ventured the assertion that 'Scots Law as it stands gives us a picture of what will some day be the law of the civilised nations,—namely a combination between the Anglo-Saxon system and the Continental system'. Whether we agree with that forecast or not, it is a striking appraisal of what Scotland has achieved, and might yet achieve.

The difficulty is that times are hard and Scotland is small, and this is not the day of small things. Even the overhead cost of the production of reports and legal works, without which any legal system must rapidly wither, is becoming a serious matter for a country where the turnover is necessarily restricted. For many practitioners the *res angusta domi* compels increasingly close application to the daily task and oblivion to the wider horizons. The fertilising foreign contacts, upon which Scots Law has thrived for ages, can only with difficulty be maintained, and there is a visible risk that the old breadth of vision may be succeeded by an insular parochialism and a disposition to rest content without inherited capital of ideas. The dangers of these tendencies are appreciated within the legal profession, and they can and will be resisted. If they were not, the future of Scots Law would soon lie behind it.

But this pamphlet is addressed not to the legal profession but to the lay citizen of Scotland, for he has an interest at stake and a part to play. Let us be frank. For some time past law and lawyers have declined in popular estimation, having become associated in the public mind with the merely traditional and reactionary. Perhaps we lawyers are in some measure to blame, in so far as we have yielded to the temptation to make law an end in itself instead of an instrument for the service of society. But the main danger to Scots Law is a different one. The spirit of the age has manifested itself in one of those recurrent crazes for the sinking of differences, the obliteration of individual characteristics, and the absorption of small units in ever larger amalgamations, as if a special virtue resided in mere size. To this there has been added an epidemic outbreak of the itch for change—what Hale described long ago as 'a certain restlessness and nauseousness in what we have and a giddy humour after somewhat which is new'. There are fields of human enterprise in which such tendencies may be allowed full play in the knowledge that they will surely issue in salutary reforms; but private law is not one of them. Their wholesale application to Scots Law could only mean its fusion with Anglo-American law, and this would involve the swift annihilation of what is left of Scotland's independent life and culture. Is that what Scotland wants? No one imagines that there exists amongst English lawyers any conscious desire to interfere with Scots Law; for the first article of the English lawyer's creed is that English Law is so incomparably superior to other systems that the others are hardly worth a glance, and there are few subjects on which England is so contentedly ignorant as Scotland and her institutions. The truth is that law is the reflection of the spirit of a people, and so long as the Scots are conscious that they are a people, they must preserve their law.

It is possible to take a higher and more universal ground. In these anxious times the sole remaining guarantee of the liberty of the subject and the freedom of a nation is the Rule of Law—that all government should be conducted, and all coercive power applied, only in obedience to pre-established principles, fixed and announced beforehand, the application of which to any given situation is capable of prediction. Unless a system of law and legal administration is maintained in a state of high efficiency and allowed to develop freely in harmony with its own distinctive principles and methods, the Rule of Law in that country will inevitably languish, and it will be the ordinary citizen who will be the victim.

The Scottish people have thus good cause to place supreme value upon their system of jurisprudence, and to promote by their interest and support every effort to preserve its unique individuality and to perfect it in its future service of the common purposes of Scottish society.

LORD COOPER

LORD COOPER OF CULROSS

Thomas Mackay Cooper was educated at George Watson's College and Edinburgh University and was called to the Scottish Bar in 1915, being made a KC in 1927. As an MP he was appointed Solicitor General in 1931 and Lord Advocate in 1935. In 1941 he was appointed Lord Justice-Clerk and became Lord Justice General in 1947, an office which he held with great distinction until his retirement in 1954. In that year he was made a Life Peer.

He made numerous contributions to legal and historical publications and was honoured by many Universities and Societies in Scotland and abroad. He died on 15 July 1955.

Afterword:
Prospects for the Future

LORD DERVAIRD

Throughout my professional career there have been voices prophesying
or urging the end of an auld sang. The times, it is said, are against the
survival of Scots law as an independent system. Nowhere are the
pressures more evident than in relation to the commercial law of this
country. Between the Scylla of English law and the Charybdis of the
law of the European Economic Community, is there any place for Scots
law? Siren voices suggest that Scots businessmen and Scots businesses
have enough difficulties to compete with in getting an adequate share of
the world's trade without the incubus of a different legal system. But the
logic can hardly stop there. If Scots law as an independent entity were to
become limited to the irreducibly territorial such as family and
succession law, some crime and (perhaps) land law, would a separate
legal tradition be worth maintaining? For law so reduced could be
regarded, and perhaps rightly regarded, as marginalised close to the
point of irrelevance. If all that was left were the not proven verdict and
the somewhat elusive concept of corroboration to distinguish Scots law
from English law would it be worth keeping?

Scotland is a small country, and the fact must frankly be faced that the
centralising effects, whether intended or not, of all governments since
the war (and doubtless long before) have removed from the commercial
and hence the legal life of Scotland much that might reasonably have
been expected to have operated from there and subject to Scots law.
When Lord Cooper wrote the first edition of this pamphlet it was not
yet perhaps apparent what effect nationalisation was to have by way of
the anglicisation of commercial law. More recently and obviously there
has been a constant stream of company takeovers and mergers which has
almost always resulted in control being vested outside Scotland. If one
asks which daily newspaper, especially of those which most protest their
'Scottishness', is actually controlled ultimately by a Scottish company,

the answer must be a melancholy one. That will do very well as an example of the extent to which economic control has passed to another legal system. To some involved in the due administration of commercial life in the United Kingdom, Scots law appears at best an irrelevance and at worst a nuisance. So when the Financial Services Act 1986 was passed, no provision was made for the regulatory boards which largely police the working of that Act to be subject to the jurisdiction of the Scottish courts (a matter corrected by the Companies Act 1989). It is symptomatic of a trend of official thinking.

And yet, and yet . . . Despite these harsh facts, in other respects the situation has been transformed since Lord Cooper wrote, in ways which give grounds for great optimism. In a small jurisdiction the life of the law must depend pre-eminently on the efforts of a few dedicated men. Thanks to the initiative of the Scottish Universities' Law Institute supported by the Carnegie Trust, there has come into existence a wide range of excellent legal work covering large tracts of law, many of which had lacked any adequate treatment for fifty years or more. Other excellent works across a wide range have been published. Now more than for a century the student and practitioner of Scots law, and the interested layman, have access to a wide range of material. In the first edition Lord Cooper referred to certain great Scots judges (to whom his own name should be added) as indicative of the strength of the Scottish legal tradition. Of far greater importance in recent times in bringing Scots law before a wider public and treating it in a systematic manner has been the work of Professor Walker and Sir Thomas Smith. Scots law has owed much of its capacity to survive these last two centuries to the institutional writers of the seventeenth and eighteenth centuries who made of it a coherent whole. By the breadth and scope of their work these latter day writers have restored vitality to Scots law. As these words are written, *The Laws of Scotland: Stair Encyclopaedia* proceeds towards completion as a worthy memorial to Sir Thomas Smith.

One peculiar difficulty that Scots law faces is the lack of direct access to a legislature in order that necessary reforms be carried through; and that has to be taken with the fact that in a small jurisdiction the capricious nature of litigation may delay or postpone indefinitely opportunities for judicial creativity in areas where the law is in need of modernisation. The Scottish Law Commission has operated to remedy the latter defect in the way of law reform and governments have been generally swift to put its proposals into law.

At the present time forces for change are developing through the legal profession. Much will change, not necessarily all for the good. But opportunities for Scots law and Scots lawyers exist in a manner undreamt of forty years ago. The distinguished tenure of the Presidency of the European Court of Justice by Lord Mackenzie Stuart and the presence there of Judge Edward ensure that Scots law will play an appropriate role in the development of the law of the EEC. Indeed its intermediate position between the two main legal systems makes it well placed to do so. Paradoxically, the extent of the pressure from the EEC for harmonisation may relieve the threat of English domination to the point of extinction of Scots law. Within the Community it is English law which is the law of the minority. The international contacts now enjoyed by Scots lawyers at many levels, and to an extent hardly contemplated even a decade ago, can only be helpful for the further development of our law. It can truly be said of the Scots lawyer of the present day that he must perforce be a comparative lawyer. Scots law does not always come out favourably from such comparison, and we must show a willingness to adapt where appropriate. If we do not, the retreat into parochialism will begin, or as some would have it, will continue. If we do, the opportunities for Scots law are, almost literally, limitless.

In the end whether there is a future for Scots law will depend mainly on the respect and affection it engenders in the people of Scotland. It is a symbol, and I venture to think the pre-eminent symbol, of the existence of Scotland as a separate nation. More than that it is the sole unifying factor which binds all Scots together. If the Scottish legal system cannot adequately serve the interests of all Scots and all of Scotland then it does not deserve to survive as a separate system of law. The intrinsic merit of Scots law and the skill and enthusiasm of those who teach and practise it have been shown over the last generation. If the impetus built up over that period can be maintained and enhanced the future for Scots law will indeed be bright. The task will not always be easy but it deserves the constant vigilance and support of all of us, laymen and lawyers alike.

MacCormick v Lord Advocate

Lord Cooper's major legacy to the Scottish legal tradition is in his many reported decisions made whilst sitting as a presiding judge in the Divisions of the Inner House of the Court of Session. Lord Cooper is generally recognised to be one of the finest thinkers ever to sit on the Scottish bench and his decisions continue to command especially high respect in the courts. As an illustration of Lord Cooper's unique style it was decided to include in this book one of his most famous opinions, that in *MacCormick v Lord Advocate*.

The full report of this case may be found in 1953 S. C. 396 and arose out of an action raised by the late John MacCormick, who was then leader of the Scottish Covenant movement, a home rule organisation which flourished in the post-war era. Briefly the facts were as follows. On the accession of the present Queen Scottish sensibilities had been offended when it was announced that Her Majesty would be styled 'Elizabeth II'. The problem was that as a matter of historical fact Elizabeth I was Queen of England *alone* and accordingly there could therefore logically be no Elizabeth II of Scotland or even, to use the monarch's correct legal style, of the United Kingdom of Great Britain and Northern Ireland. So strong was feeling on this matter that the issue was eventually brought to court in an attempt to persuade the Court of Session to forbid the use of the offensive numeral in Scotland. The legal dilemma which confronted the court on this issue was acute because the offending royal style had been given the force of law by an act of parliament, the Royal Titles Act 1953, but on the other hand there were the brute unalterable fact that there had never been an Elizabeth I of Great Britain and the argument that the style breached the Treaty of Union of 1707.

S.C.S.

LORD PRESIDENT (Cooper). This is a petition of suspension and interdict against the Lord Advocate, as representing Her Majesty's Ministers and Officers of State, praying for interdict against them from publishing a proclamation entitling Her Majesty as, *inter alia*, 'Elizabeth the Second of the United Kingdom of Great Britain.' Some of the questions which would have arisen as to the feasibility of such a remedy were largely superseded by the petitioners' invocation of section 21 of the Crown Proceedings Act, 1947,[1] in terms of which they asked only for 'an order declaratory of the rights of parties'. Where such an order is asked, I consider that it should be formulated with precision, and this has not been done. But it was made sufficiently plain in the pleadings and argument that what the petitioners sought was a finding from this Court that the use in Her Majesty's title of 'the numeral' was not only inconsistent with historical fact and political reality, but involved a contravention of the Treaty of Union of 1707 and of the relative Scottish and English legislation passed at that time.

The Lord Ordinary dismissed the petition upon these grounds: (1) that the adoption of 'the numeral' had been expressly authorised by the Royal Titles Act, 1953,[2] and that an Act of the Parliament of Great Britain was not challengeable in any Court as being in breach of the Treaty of Union or on any other ground; (2) that in any event article 1 of the Treaty did not expressly or by implication prohibit the use of 'the numeral', and that the action therefore failed on relevancy; and (3) that the petitioners had no legal title or interest to sue.

In the first place, the argument has not satisfied me that the Royal Titles Act, 1953,[2] has any proper bearing upon the sole issue here in controversy. That Act only received the Royal Assent on 26th March 1953. More than thirteen months previously, on 6th February 1952, Her Majesty was proclaimed at her Accession Council (and immediately thereafter throughout the Realm and the Dominions) under the name of 'Elizabeth the Second'. It was under the same name and 'numeral' that Her Majesty on 8th February 1952 subscribed the statutory oath in relation to the rights and privileges of the Church of Scotland. We have judicial knowledge of these facts because the original oath, together with the relative Instrument and Order in Council, was presented to this

---

[1] 10 and 11 Geo. VI, cap. 44.
[2] 1 and 2 Eliz. II, cap. 9.

Court on 12 February 1952, and was directed to be recorded in the Books of Sederunt and to be transmitted to the Keeper of the Records of Scotland. Identical procedure *mutatis mutandis* was followed on the occasion of the accession of Their Majesties Edward VII, George V, Edward VIII and George VI. In all these instances the name and 'the numeral' were adopted without the authority of any Act of Parliament (anticipatory or retrospective), and were never altered during the reigns of the several sovereigns concerned. There have been several statutes in the last 150 years dealing with the 'royal style and titles', but it is plain from an examination of them and of the royal proclamations which followed that each and all were concerned not with the name and the 'numeral' but with the appendant designations and with the necessity for varying those appendant designations because of some supervening change in the status of some part of the territories still or previously acknowledging allegiance to the British Crown—notably the differing positions at different times of Ireland, India and what are now the Dominions. The Act of 1953 is, in my view, in the same general category as the earlier Acts of this type, its occasion (as the preamble discloses) being a meeting with the Dominion representatives in December 1952. There is however this significant difference, that the Act of 1953 merely signifies the 'assent' of the United Kingdom Parliament to the adoption of unspecified styles and titles, whereas the earlier Acts (notably those passed in 1876, 1901, 1927 and 1947) bore to authorise the alteration by the expression 'it shall be lawful for Her (or His) Majesty'. The proclamation issued on 28th May 1953 in pursuance of the Act of 1953 substitutes 'Northern Ireland' for 'Ireland'; alters the formula applicable to the Commonwealth and Empire overseas; but leaves the name and the 'numeral' and the rest of the style and title unaffected. I find it impossible to hold that the Act of 1953 authorised, either retrospectively or by anticipation, the adoption by Her Majesty of the name and 'numeral' by which she was initially proclaimed and has ever since been officially known.

I interpose this observation, that, if it were necessary to construe the Act of 1953, I should find it impossible to do so because the Act is not self-contained. All the other Acts dealing with a change in the royal style and titles simply authorised the sovereign to adopt such changed styles and titles as the sovereign might think fit. But in 1953 the sovereign's discretion in the matter is not unqualified. The changed style and titles to which Parliament assented must be such as Her Majesty may think fit *'having regard to the said Agreement'*. What agreement? Plainly the agreement said to have been concluded with the Dominion representatives in December 1952. But this agreement is not scheduled or otherwise detailed, the only reference to it being in the vague words of the preamble of the Act, which are entirely lacking in specification. The Lord Advocate admitted that the Act was not self-explanatory, and offered in supplement a 'White Paper', which he indicated had been made available in the Vote Office prior to the consideration of the bill. But Parliament can only speak through the medium of a statute. A Court of law is not entitled to investigate the Parliamentary history of a bill, whether in the pages of Hansard or in their equivalent, a 'White Paper', and I am therefore forced to the conclusion that this Act must remain incapable of being fully understood or intelligently interpreted by any Court, the Legislature having withheld the material necessary for that purpose. Be that as it may, I consider that the Lord Advocate failed to show that there is, or ever was, Parliamentary authority for the adoption by Her Majesty of the name and the 'numeral' which in fact were adopted on Her Majesty's accession and have been used ever since.

Upon this view a part of the Lord Ordinary's judgment and of the argument before us disappears. But lest this case should go further, I shall briefly express my opinion.

The principle of the unlimited sovereignty of Parliament is a distinctively English principle which has no counterpart in Scottish constitutional law. It derives its origin from Coke and Blackstone, and was widely popularised during the nineteenth century by Bagehot and Dicey, the latter having stated the doctrine in its classic form in his Law of the Constitution. Considering that the Union legislation extinguished the Parliaments of Scotland and England and replaced them by a new Parliament, I have difficulty in seeing why it should have been supposed that the new Parliament of Great Britain must inherit all the peculiar characteristics of the English Parliament but none of the Scottish Parliament, as if all that happened in 1707 was that Scottish representatives were admitted to the Parliament of England. That is not what was done. Further, the Treaty and the associated legislation, by which the Parliament of Great Britain was brought into being as the successor of the separate Parliaments of Scotland and England, contain some clauses which expressly reserve to the Parliament of Great Britain powers of subsequent modification, and other clauses which either contain no such power or emphatically exclude subsequent alteration by

98

declarations that the provision shall be fundamental and unalterable in all time coming, or declarations of a like effect. I have never been able to understand how it is possible to reconcile with elementary canons of construction the adoption by the English constitutional theorists of the same attitude to these markedly different types of provisions.

The Lord Advocate conceded this point by admitting that the Parliament of Great Britain 'could not' repeal or alter such 'fundamental and essential' conditions. He was doubtless influenced in making this concession by the modified views expressed by Dicey in his later work entitled Thoughts on the Scottish Union, from which I take this passage (pp. 252–253): 'The statesmen of 1707, though giving full sovereign power to the Parliament of Great Britain, clearly believed in the possibility of creating an absolutely sovereign Legislature which should yet be bound by unalterable laws.' After instancing the provisions as to Presbyterian Church government in Scotland with their emphatic prohibition against alteration, the author proceeds: 'It represents the conviction of the Parliament which passed the Act of Union that the Act for the security of the Church of Scotland ought to be morally or constitutionally unchangeable, even by the British Parliament . . . A sovereign Parliament, in short, though it cannot be logically bound to abstain from changing any given law, may, by the fact that an Act when it was passed had been declared to be unchangeable, receive a warning that it cannot be changed without grave danger to the Constitution of the country.' I have not found in the Union legislation any provision that the Parliament of Great Britain should be 'absolutely sovereign' in the sense that that Parliament should be free to alter the Treaty at will. However that may be, these passages provide a necessary corrective to the extreme formulations adopted by the Lord Ordinary, and not now supported. In the latest editions of the Law of the Constitution the editor uneasily describes Dicey's theories as 'purely lawyer's conceptions', and demonstrates how deeply later events, such as the Statute of Westminster, have encroached upon the earlier dogmas. As is well known, the conflict between academic logic and political reality has been emphasised by the recent South African decision as to the effect of the Statute of Westminster—Harris v Minister of Interior.[1]

But the petitioners have still a grave difficulty to overcome on this branch of their argument. Accepting it that there are provisions in the Treaty of Union and associated legislation which are 'fundamental law',

[1] [1952] 1 T. L. R. 1245.

and assuming for the moment that something is alleged to have been done—it matters not whether with legislative authority or not—in breach of that fundamental law, the question remains whether such a question is determinable as a justiciable issue in the Courts of either Scotland or England, in the same fashion as an issue of constitutional *vires* would be cognisable by the Supreme Courts of the United States, or of South Africa or Australia. I reserve my opinion with regard to the provisions relating expressly to this Court and to the laws 'which concern private right' which are administered here. This is not such a question, but a matter of 'public right' (articles 18 and 19). To put the matter in another way, it is of little avail to ask whether the Parliament of Great Britain 'can' do this thing or that, without going on to inquire who can stop them if they do. Any person 'can' repudiate his solemn engagement but he cannot normally do so with impunity. Only two answers have been suggested to this corollary to the main question. The first is the exceedingly cynical answer implied by Dicey (Law of the Constitution (9th ed.) p. 82) in the statement that 'it would be rash of the Imperial Parliament to abolish the Scotch law courts, and assimilate the law of Scotland to that of England. But no one can feel sure at which point Scottish resistance to such a change would become serious.' The other answer was that nowadays there may be room for the invocation of an 'advisory opinion' from the International Court of Justice. On these matters I express no view. This at least is plain, that there is neither precedent nor authority of any kind for the view that the domestic Courts of either Scotland or England have jurisdiction to determine whether a governmental act of the type here in controversy is or is not conform to the provisions of a Treaty, least of all when that Treaty is one under which both Scotland and England ceased to be independent states and merged their identity in an incorporating union. From the standpoint both of constitutional law and of international law the position appears to me to be unique, and I am constrained to hold that the action as laid is incompetent in respect that it has not been shown that the Court of Session has authority to entertain the issue sought to be raised.

Upon the question of the relevancy of the petitioners' averments of breach of the provisions of the Treaty I agree in the result with the Lord Ordinary. Only article 1 of the Treaty was founded upon, and it was conceded that there was nothing explicit in that article dealing with the point in controversy. I am unable to find in that article any sufficient implied prohibition against the adoption of the 'numeral' complained of, and this view is supported by the practice of 120 years. That practice is doubtless correctly explained in Phillips's Principles of English Law and the Constitution (1939) (at pp. 229–230) as follows: 'The number attached to the name of a king refers to the Kings of *England* since the Norman conquest'; for, if this is not the rule, all the kings of the name of Edward since Edward I have been wrongly numbered. Whether the rule is good or bad, and whether it is politically wise to continue to apply it, it is not for this Court to say; but, in so far as I am entitled to look at article 1 of the Treaty, I am unable to affirm that any breach has been committed.

Finally, I agree with the Lord Ordinary on title to sue. There is no plea by the respondent to this point and it is of minor significance. It is true that we in Scotland recognise within certain limits the *actio popularis*, in which any member of the public may be entitled as such to vindicate certain forms of public right. But the device has never been extended to such a case as this. I cannot see how we could admit the title and interest of the present petitioners to raise the point in issue before the Court of Session without conceding a similar right to almost any opponent of almost any political action to which public opposition has arisen.

For these reasons, which differ in certain respects from the views expressed by the Lord Ordinary, I am for adhering to his Lordship's interlocutor. I desire to place it on record that the petitioners expressly disclaimed any attempt to criticise Her Majesty or any disloyalty to Her, their action being based upon considerations of which the present issue is merely symbolical.

THE STAIR SOCIETY: AN INTRODUCTION

THE STAIR SOCIETY was founded in 1934 to encourage the study and advance the knowledge of the history of Scots Law. Since then it has published 37 volumes, including an Introduction to Scottish Legal History, Hope's and Balfour's Practicks, a Formulary of Old Scots Legal Documents, and a study of the 19th-century reforms of the Court of Session. A new supplementary series has begun with Professor Hannay's essays on the early history of that court. The Society aims to produce a volume each year, though this is not guaranteed.

In making knowledge of the past more readily accessible the Society depends on the support of Scottish lawyers, students of Scots law, and all interested in Scotland's distinctive legal tradition.

A list of past publications available for purchase and any further information desired can be obtained from the Secretary, Mr Ivor R. Guild, CBE, WS, 16 Charlotte Square, Edinburgh EH2 4YS.

Enrolment Form overleaf

STAIR SOCIETY ENROLMENT FORM

The present subscription rates are:

Individual members £12.00
Institutional Members £15.00
Student Members £6.00

USA and CANADA
Individual Members $30.00
Institutional Members $35.00

Please enrol me as a member of The Stair Society. Enclosed is a remittance for £........... [Institutions £..........] in payment of my first subscription.

Please send me details of availability of earlier volumes.

NAME ....

ADDRESS ....

....

....

In the case of institutions add:

Full title of institution: ....

....

Address for communications: ....

....

....

Date ....

When completed please send form to Ivor R. Guild, CBE, WS, Secretary, The Stair Society, 16 Charlotte Square, Edinburgh EH2 4YS.